Ready for My Close-up!

OTHER WORKS BY DENNY MARTIN FLINN

Non-Fiction:

Little Musicals for Little Theaters: A Guide to the Musicals That Don't Need Chandeliers and Helicopters to Succeed

How Not to Audition

How Not to Write a Screenplay

Musical! A Grand Tour: The Rise, Glory and Fall of an American Institution

What They Did for Love: The Untold Story Behind the Making of the Broadway Musical A Chorus Line

Novels:

San Francisco Kills (a Spencer Holmes Mystery)

Killer Finish (a Spencer Holmes Mystery)

The Fearful Summons (a Star Trek novel)

Screenplay:

Star Trek VI: The Undiscovered Country (co-author)

Ready for My Close-up!

GREAT MOVIE SPEECHES

Compiled by Denny Martin Flinn

LIMELIGHT EDITIONS
An Imprint of Hal Leonard Corporation
New York

Published in 2007 by Limelight Editions
An Imprint of Hal Leonard Corporation
19 West 21st Street, New York, NY 10010

Printed in the United States of America

Book design by Lesley Kunikis

Library of Congress Cataloging-in-Publication Data is available upon request.

ISBN-10: 0-87910-350-7
ISBN-13: 978-0-87910-350-7

www.limelighteditions.com

For the writers . . .

I can't go on with the scene. I'm too happy. Do you mind, Mr. DeMille, if I say a few words? Thank you. I just want to tell you how happy I am to be back in the studio, making a picture again. You don't know how much I've missed all of you. And I promise you I'll never desert you again, because after Salome we'll make another picture, and another and another. You see, this is my life. It always will be. There's nothing else—just us and the camera and those wonderful people out there in the dark . . . All right, Mr. DeMille, I'm ready for my close-up.

—**Norma Desmond** (*Sunset Boulevard*)

CONTENTS

Chapter 4: Places

Chapter 5: War and Peace

On the Frontier

World War I

World War II

The Cold War

Chapter 7: Issues

Chapter 8: Stories

Chapter 9: Hollywood

Chapter 10: The Theatre

Chapter 11: Romance

Chapter 12: Other Passions

Chapter 13: Back to the Future

Epilogue

Credits

Text and Photograph Permissions

INTRODUCTION

"If I want to send a message, I'll call Western Union."

This famous line has been attributed to various movie moguls, particularly Samuel Goldwyn, but probably originated with George S. Kaufman. In any case, about the time it was first uttered, movies were in the midst of a golden age of dialogue. Films included more messages, ideas, themes, moral essays, and pontifications than they have since.

During the moguls' reign over the studio system, producers and directors—even the stars—trembled at any commands from the front office, while the low men and women on the totem pole—the screenwriters—went quietly to their typewriters and, in the best tradition of the subversive revolutionaries that most writers are, turned out reams of dialogue that did send messages. How could they resist? They had the biggest and best platform in the world: Hollywood movies.

The speeches collected here are culled from some of the best, and a few of the worst, films ever made. It's hardly a definitive collection. If I've omitted your favorite speech, my apologies. Nor is there ever a definitive version. Wherever possible I've relied on the published versions or manuscript drafts. These don't always include changes that were made late in production by actors or directors. I have tried to be loyal to the writers. (Once upon a time George Kaufman posted a notice on the callboard for one of his plays: "Rehearsal tomorrow morning at ten o'clock to take out the improvements.")

"Speeches," as opposed to "monologues," are less about emotions than ideas. There's little here that could impress a casting director. These are the speeches the writers created as much for themselves as for their characters. Besides sheer eloquence, possibly a lost art in screenwriting today, they have in common a passion for political and social, economic and emotional, ideas, and the wit and wisdom to express them. Here in speeches long and short, subdued and volatile, are the great screenwriters' themes of the twentieth century.

—DMF

CHAPTER 1:
Philosophies

AMERICAN REPUBLIC

When the real Davy Crockett was asked to help defend The Alamo *with his Tennessee volunteers, his explanation probably wasn't as eloquent as John Wayne's. But "when the fact becomes legend, print the legend."*

Davy Crockett: "Republic." I like the sound of the word. Means people can live free. Talk free. Go or come, buy or sell, be drunk or sober, however they choose. Some words give you a feeling. "Republic" is one of those words that makes me tight in the throat. Same tightness a man gets when a baby takes his first step, or his first baby shaves and makes his first sound like a man. Some words can give you a feeling that makes your heart warm. "Republic" is one of those words.

THE CHURCH OF BASEBALL

Sports are rich with "Baseball Annies," the women who attach themselves to players. This one from Bull Durham *explains herself.*

Annie Savoy: I believe in the church of baseball. I tried all the major religions and most of the minor ones. I've worshipped Buddha, Allah, Brahma, Vishnu, trees, mushrooms, and Isadora Duncan. I know things. For instance, there are one hundred eight beads in a Catholic rosary and one hundred eight stitches on a baseball. When I learned that, I gave Jesus a chance. But it just didn't work out between us. The Lord laid too much guilt on me. I prefer metaphysics to theology. You see, there's no guilt in baseball, and it's never boring, which makes it like sex. There's never been a ball player who's slept with me who didn't have the best year of his career. Making love is like hitting a baseball—you just got to relax and concentrate. Besides, I'd never sleep with a player hitting under .250 unless he had a lot of RBI's and was a great glove man up the middle. You see, there's a certain amount of life wisdom I give these boys. Sometimes when I've got a ball player alone, I'll just read Emily Dickinson or Walt Whitman to him. And the guys are so sweet, they always stay and listen. Of course, a guy will listen to anything if he thinks its foreplay. I make them feel confident and they make me feel safe and pretty. Of course, what I give them lasts a lifetime. What they give me lasts one hundred forty-two games. Sometimes that seems like a bad trade, but bad trades are part of baseball. Who can forget Frank Robinson or Milt Pappas, for God's sake? It's a long season, and you gotta trust it. I've tried them all, I really have, and the only church that truly feeds the soul is the church of baseball.

I BELIEVE IN PUSSY

This year's chosen player, however, has some pretty strong ideas of his own.

Crash: Well, I believe in the soul. The cock. The pussy. The small of a woman's back. The hanging curve ball. High fiber. Good scotch. That the novels of Susan Sontag are self-indulgent, overrated crap. I believe Lee Harvey Oswald acted alone. I believe there ought to be a constitutional amendment outlawing Astroturf and the designated hitter. I believe in the sweet spot, soft-core pornography, opening your presents Christmas morning rather than Christmas Eve. And I believe in long, slow, deep, soft, wet kisses that last three days. Goodnight.

PEP TALK

In football on Any Given Sunday, *any team can win. This coach thinks it's just a question of who wants it badly enough.*

Tony D'Amato: I don't know what to say really. Three minutes to the biggest battle of our professional lives all comes down to today. Now, either we heal as a team or we're gonna crumble. Inch by inch, play by play—till we're finished. We're in hell right now, gentleman. Believe me. And we can stay here, get the shit kicked out of us, or we can fight our way back, into the light. We can climb out of hell, one inch at a time. Now, I can't do it for you, I'm too old. I look around I see these young faces and I think, I mean, I made every wrong choice a middle-aged man can make. I pissed away all my money, believe it or not, I chased off anyone who's ever loved me, and lately I can't even stand the face I see in the mirror. Y'know, when you get old in life things get taken from you; that's part of life. But you only learn that when you start losin' stuff. You find out life's this game of inches, and so is football. Because, in either game, life, or football, the margin for error is so small. I mean, one half a step too late or too early, and you don't quite make it. One half-second too slow or too fast, you don't quite catch it. The inches we need are everywhere around us. They're in every break in the game, every minute, every second. On this team we fight for that inch. On this team we tear ourselves and everyone else around us to pieces for that inch. We claw with our fingernails for that inch. Because we know when we add up all those inches, that's going to make the fucking difference between winning and losing. Between living and dying. I'll tell you this: in any fight it's the guy who's willing to die who's gonna win that inch. And I know that if I'm going to have any life anymore, it's because I'm still willing to fight and die for that inch. Because that's what living is: the six inches in front of your face. Now, I can't make you do it. You gotta look at the guy next to you, look into his eyes. Now I think you're gonna see a guy who will go that inch with you. You're gonna see a guy who will sacrifice himself for this team because he knows when it comes down to it, you're going to do the same for him. That's a team, gentlemen, and either we heal now as a team or we will die as individuals. That's football, guys. That's all it is. Now, what are you going to do?

MORE FOOTBALL

A football coach recruited by St. Anthony's College wants to make sure that the Father recruiting him knows what he's in for. There could be Trouble Along the Way.

Steve Aloysius Williams: Oh, it's a great game, football. Noble game. Originated in England in 1823, when an enterprising young man named William Webb Ellis—who studied for the ministry, by the way—found his team behind in a soccer game. So he picked up the ball and ran through the amazed opponents for a thoroughly illegal touchdown. And that's how football was born. Illegitimately. So it moved to America where someone took advantage of a loophole in the rules and created a little formation called the flying wedge. So many young men were maimed and killed by this clever maneuver that President Roosevelt—Theodore Roosevelt—had to call the colleges together and asked them to make the game less brutal. He was of course defeated in the next election. In spite of this setback, football became an industry. The price of a good running back often surpassed the salary of a professor. And this committee unearthed this well-known fact: it was always the coach who took it on the chin. I just got tired of picking myself up.

ONE TRUE SELF

Eddie Jessup is researching various methods of achieving Altered States *of consciousness. What's he really looking for?*

Jessup: I'm a man in search of his true self. How archetypically American can you get? Everybody's looking for their true selves. We're all trying to fulfill ourselves, understand ourselves, get in touch with ourselves, face the reality of ourselves, explore ourselves, expand ourselves. Ever since we dispensed with God, we've got nothing but ourselves to explain this meaningless horror of life. Well, I think that true self, that original self, that first self is a real, mensurate, quantifiable thing, tangible and incarnate. And I'm going to find the fucker.

YOGA

He was unimpressed with Yoga.

Jessup: No matter how you slice it, yoga is still a state-specific technology operating in the service of an *a priori* belief system, not much different from other trance-inducing techniques. Of course, the breathing exercises are effective as hell. The breathing becomes an entity in itself, an actual state of consciousness in its own right, so that your body breathing becomes the embodiment of your breath. But it's still a renunciatory technique to achieve a predetermined trance state, what the Zen people call an "isness," a very pure narcissism, Freud's oceanic feeling. What dignifies the yoga practices is that the belief system itself is not truly religious. There is no Buddhist God, per se. It is the self, the individual mind, that contains immortality and ultimate truth.

NOTHINGNESS

He finds what he's looking for through a combination of hallucinogenic drugs and a sensory deprivation tank. Don't try this at home.

Jessup: My matter was returning to pure energy, to a condition of pure nothingness. And you saved me from nothingness. But it doesn't end there, you see. It keeps going. Beyond nothingness to something even more horrible. Beyond the physical, beyond matter, beyond energy, beyond science. You see, matter, energy, our whole universe, are not absolutes. They are all fictions of human consciousness. And there are other consciousnesses and other universes. Our space is just one space among infinite spaces. If you want to know what happens to a dying star, I can tell you—it is sucked into another universe, another consciousness. And if you hadn't held me in one piece, that's what would've happened to me! It is stark entropy! It is stark terror! Can you understand what I'm saying? . . . I was in it, Emily! I was in that ultimate moment of terror that is the beginning of life. I found the final truth! I found it, touched it, ate of its flesh, drank of its blood! I've seen it face to face, and it is hideous! It is insufferable! The pain cannot be described! It is nothing, simple, hideous nothing! The final truth of all things is that there is no final truth! Truth is what's transitory! It's human life that is real! You and me sitting here in this room! That is real! That is the only truth there is! I don't want to frighten you, Emily, but what I'm trying to tell you is that that moment of terror is not just a philosophical concept to me. It's a real and living horror, living and growing within me now, eating my flesh, drinking of my blood. It's real because I have made it real. It's alive. It's in me. It is me. And the only thing that keeps it from devouring me is you.

Emily: I think you're trying to tell me you love me.

THE UNSPEAKABLE TERROR

He is. She has a better way of saying it.

Emily: My God, do you think you're the only one who has experienced despair? The only one who has felt the utter nothingness of life? We are all creatures of despair, Eddie. Life for all of us is a flight from the unspeakable terror! Life is an act of faith for all of us! That's why we love each other! It's the only act of faith most of us are capable of! At least, it's the only act of faith I'm capable of! We all live with it. That unspeakable terror is what makes us such singular creatures. We hide from it, we flee from it, we succumb to it, mostly we defy it! We build fragile little structures to keep it out. We love, we raise families, we work, we make friends. We write poems, we paint pictures, we build beautiful things. We make our own universe, our own truth, we believe in our own reality. And every now and then, someone like you comes along who goes out and challenges it face to face. Passionate men. Poets, philosophers, saints, and scientists. What the hell do you think makes me love you so much?

IT'S ALL SHIT

Awash in a Sea of Love, *this cop takes time out to explain how the world really works.*

Frank: Look, a lot of guys on the job, we see a lot of shit. A lot of suffering. Every day. It's like in the beginning, one time when I was in uniform, I get this call. We break into this apartment. A four-year-old kid is chained to the radiator. The mother's somewheres scoring dope, who knows. We take the kid to a hospital, wait for the mother to come home. I start chasing this bitch around the block. We bust her for child abuse, abandonment. I'm freakin' six ways to Sunday, but my partner, older guy, he says, "Hey, Frank, let me tell you something. That lady? She's a piece of shit. But ten years ago, I busted her *father* for child abuse. He *was* a piece of shit. This kid we saved tonight? If he lives long enough, he's *gonna* be a piece of shit. It's the cycle of shit and there's nothing to do for it, so relax."

DON'T LET THIS COUNTRY GO TO THE DEVIL

Seven years of prosperity were granted farmer Jabez Stone in exchange for—what else?—his soul. When the devil (Mr. Scratch) comes to collect, however, the farmer gets himself a good lawyer, and the stage is set for a courtroom showdown between The Devil and Daniel Webster.

Webster: Gentlemen of the jury: It is my privilege to be addressing tonight a group of men I've long been acquainted with in song and story, but men I had never hoped to see. My worthy opponent, Mr. Scratch, has called you Americans all, and Mr. Scratch was right—you are Americans all! Oh, what a heritage you were born to share! Gentlemen of the jury, I envy you! For you were there at the *birth* of the mighty Union. It was given to you to hear those first cries of pain—and to behold the shining babe that was born of blood and tears. Tonight, you are called upon to judge a man named Jabez Stone. What is his case? He is accused of breach of contract—He made a deal to find a short cut in his life—to get rich quickly. The same deal all of you once made. You, Benedict Arnold! I speak to you first, because you're better known than all your other colleagues here. What a different song yours *could* have been! A friend of Washington and LaFayette—a *soldier*—General Arnold, you fought so gallantly for the American cause, till—What was the date? Oh, yes—in 1779, a date burned in your heart. The lure of gold made you betray that cause. You, Simon Girty, now known to us as *Renegade*! A loathsome word—you also took that other way. *You*, Walter Butler—What would you give to have another chance to let the grasses grow in Cherry Valley without the stain of blood? You, Captain Kidd and you, Governor Dale—I could go on and name you all, but there's no need of that. Why stir the wounds? I know they pain enough. All of you were fooled like Jabez Stone—fooled and trapped in your desire to rebel against your fate. Gentlemen of the jury, it's the eternal right of man to raise his fist against his fate, but every time he does, he stands at a crossroads. You took the wrong turn and so did Jabez Stone. But he found out in time. He is here tonight to save his soul. Gentlemen of the jury, I ask that you give Jabez Stone another chance to walk upon the earth, among— the trees, the growing corn, the smell of grass in spring. What would you give for one more chance to see those things that you must all remember and often long to feel again? For you were all men once. Clean American air was in your lungs—you breathed it deep, for it was free and blew across an earth you loved. These are common things I speak of, small things, but they are good things. Yet without your soul they are nothing. Without your soul they sicken. Mr. Scratch told you that your soul is nothing and you believed him. It has cost you your freedom. Freedom is not just a big word; it is the bread and the morning and the risen sun. It was for freedom we came in boats and ships to these shores. It has been a long journey, a hard one, a bitter one. There is sadness in being a man, but it is a proud thing, too. Out of the suffering and the starvation, the wrong and the right, a new thing has come—a free man. When the ships of the oppressors are broken, and their names forgotten and destroyed, free men will be walking and talking under a free star. Yes, we have planted freedom here in this earth like wheat. We have said to the sky above us, "A man shall own his own soul." Now, here is this man. He is your brother! You are Americans all, you cannot (pointing at the Devil) take his side—the side of the oppressor. Let Jabez Stone keep his soul—this soul which doesn't belong to him alone, which belongs to his son—his family—his country. Gentlemen of the jury—

don't let this country go to the devil! Free Jabez Stone! God save the United States and the men who have made her free!

A POSTER CHILD FOR THE NEXT MILLENNIUM

The Devil's Advocate *gets his turn. Head of a multi-national corporation of— what else?—lawyers, his first speech seems to blame human evolution on God.*

John Milton: Eddie Barzoon! Eddie Barzoon! Ha! I nursed him through two divorces, a cocaine rehab, and a pregnant receptionist. God's creature, right? God's special creature? Ha! And I've warned him, Kevin, I've warned him every step of the way. Watching him bounce around like a fucking game, like a wind-up toy! Like 250 pounds of self-serving greed on wheels! The next thousand years is right around the corner, Kevin, and Eddie Barzoon—take a good look. Because he's the poster child for the next millennium! These people, it's no mystery where they come from. You sharpen the human appetite to the point where it could split atoms with its desire. You build egos the size of cathedrals, fiber-optically connect the world to every eager impulse, grease even the dullest dreams with these dollar-green, gold-played fantasies, until every human becomes an aspiring emperor! Becomes his own God! Where can you go from there? And as we're scrambling from one deal to the next, who's got his eye on the planet? As the air thickens, the water sours, even the bees' honey takes on the metallic taste of radioactivity, and it just keeps coming! Faster and faster! There's no chance to think, to prepare, it's "buy futures, sell futures when there is no future!" We've got a runaway train, boy! We've got a billion Eddie Barzoons all jogging into the future. Every one of them ready to fist-fuck God's ex-planet, lick their fingers clean as they reach out with their pristine cybernetic keyboards to total up their billable hours. And then it hits home! It's a little late in the game to buy out now!! Your belly's too full, your dick is sore, your eyes are bloodshot, and you're screaming for someone to help!! But guess what? There's no one there! You're all alone, Eddie!! You're God's special little creature!! Maybe it's true. Maybe God threw the dice once too often. Maybe He let us all down.

IT'S MY TURN

With his second wild oration, the Devil's Advocate *offers his son a better deal, if only the son will sell his soul, too.*

John Milton: Y'know, boy, guilt is like a bag of fucking bricks. All you gotta do is set it down. Who are you carrying all those bricks for, anyway? God? Is that it? God? Well, I'll tell ya, lemme give you a little inside information about God. God likes to watch. He's a prankster. Think about it. He gives man instincts! He gives us this extraordinary gift and then what does he do? I swear, for his own amusement, his own private cosmic gag reel, he sets the rules in opposition. It's the goof of all time. Look—but don't touch. Touch—but don't taste. Taste. Don't swallow. And while you're jumping from one foot to the next, he's laughing his sick, fucking ass off! He's a tight-ass, he's a sadist, he's an absentee landlord! Worship that? Never!

Kevin Lomax: Better to reign in Hell than serve in Heaven, is that it?

John Milton: Why not? I'm here on the ground with my nose in it since the whole thing began! I've nurtured every sensation Man has been inspired to have! I cared about what he wanted and I never judged him. Why? Because I never rejected him. In spite of all his imperfections, I'm a fan of man!! I'm a humanist. Maybe the last humanist. Who, in their right mind, Kevin, could possibly deny the twentieth century was entirely mine? All of it, Kevin, all of it! Mine. I'm peaking here. It's my time now. It's our time.

A THEORY OF EQUALITY

The man commanding The Alamo *(because, unlike in the picture, Colonel Jim Bowie was in bed with pneumonia) is something of a Southern snob, who doesn't trust his men. (It's why he lies to them about the prospect of reinforcements.)*

Colonel William Travis: I know you think my attitude incongruous with those of your idol Thomas Jefferson, the messiah of equality. You think it's snobbish of me to feel that I am better than that rabble. Tell me this: Suppose we accept the first half of your Jefferson's theory of equality and grant that all men draw their first breath as equals. Now let us project that life to the grave which awaits us all. Do you deny that most men live lives of craven compromise? Of snatching every shabby opportunity to feather their nests? To be quick to raise the call for safety, for security, while let the other man volunteer, let the other man carry the rifle, let the other man face the hard call of honor. Why, even your Mr. Jefferson, writing in his ivory tower in Monticello, had to admit that most men are like that, and only a few, unhappily a very few, go to their graves with their honor untarnished, never having grabbed for the wealth that comes with opportunism, or the popularity that comes with catering to those smelly masses. And can you, or any sane person, or your sainted Thomas Jefferson, claim that such men are no more than the equal of those creatures down below? And so I say without any conceit or snobbishness, that I am better than that rabble down there.

TWO VISIONS FOR SHANGRI-LA

Noting the general direction of the world, a small community relocates itself beyond a Lost Horizon. *Their leader explains why.*

High Lama: We have reason. It is the entire meaning and purpose of Shangri-La. It came to me in a vision, long, long, ago. I saw all the nations strengthening, not in wisdom, but in the vulgar passions and the will to destroy. I saw their machine power multiply until a single weaponed man might match a whole army. I foresaw a time when man, exulting in the technique of murder, would rage so hotly over the world that every book, every treasure, would be doomed to destruction. This vision was so vivid and so moving that I determined to gather together all the things of beauty and culture that I could and preserve them here against the doom toward which the world is rushing. Look at the world today! Is there anything more pitiful? What madness there is, what blindness, what unintelligent leadership! A scurrying mass of bewildered humanity crashing headlong against each other, propelled by an orgy of greed and brutality. The time must come, my friend, when this orgy will spend itself, when brutality and the lust for power must perish by its own sword. Against that time is why I avoided death and am here, and why you were brought here. For when that day comes, the world must begin to look for a new life. And it is our hope that they may find it here. For here we shall be with their books and their music and a way of life based on one simple rule: Be Kind. When that day comes it is our hope that the brotherly love of Shangri-La will spread throughout the world. Yes, my son, when the strong devour each other, the Christian ethic may at least be fulfilled, and the meek shall inherit the earth.

One of the High Lama's younger followers has a bit more hope for us.

Sondra: There's a wish for Shangri-La in everyone's heart. I have never seen the outside world. But I understand there are millions and millions of people who are supposed to be mean and greedy. Yet I just know that, secretly, they are all hoping to find a garden spot where there is peace and security, where there's beauty and comfort, where they wouldn't have to be mean and greedy. Oh, I just wish the whole world might come to this valley.

THEY WILL COME

Everybody has their Field of Dreams. *Ray's is a baseball stadium. But should he build one over his cornfield? This man thinks so.*

Terence Mann: Ray. People will come, Ray. They'll come to Iowa for reasons they can't even fathom. They'll turn into your driveway, not knowing for sure why they're doing it. They'll arrive at your door, as innocent as children, longing for the past. "Of course, we won't mind if you look around," you'll say, "It's only twenty dollars per person." And they'll pass over the money without even thinking about it. Whereas money they have, and peace they lack. . . And they'll walk off to the bleachers and sit in their short sleeves on a perfect afternoon. And find they have reserved seats somewhere along the baselines where they sat when they were children. And cheer their heroes. And they'll watch the game, and it'll be as if they'd dipped themselves in magic waters. The memories will be so thick they'll have to brush them away from their faces. People will come, Ray. The one constant through all the years, Ray, has been baseball. America has rolled by like an army of steamrollers. It's been erased like a blackboard, rebuilt, and erased again. But baseball has marked the time. This field, this game, is a part of our past, Ray. It reminds us of all that once was good, and that could be again. Oh, people will come, Ray. People will most definitely come.

I'LL PLAY

Here's one old player who will certainly come.

"Moonlight" Graham: Well, you know I never got to bat in the major leagues. I'd like to have my chance just once, to stare down a big league pitcher, to stare him down and, just as he goes into his wind-up, wink, make him think you know something he doesn't. That's what I wish. A chance to squint at the sky so blue that it hurts your eyes just to look at it. To feel the tingle in your arms as you connect with the ball, to run the bases, stretch a double into a triple, and flop face-first into third, wrap your arms around the bag. That's my wish, Ray Kinsella, that's my wish. And is there enough magic out there in the moonlight to make this dream come true?

WHAT IS POETRY?

English professor John Keating is determined to make poetry live for his students. He has no use for the pages of Professor Pritchard's academic deconstruction in their textbook. He requests that the students enthusiastically rip out Pritchard's pages.

Keating: Keep ripping, gentlemen! This is a battle. A war. And the casualties could be your hearts and souls. Thank you, Dalton. Armies of academics going forward, measuring poetry. No! We'll not have that here. No more Mr. J. Evans Pritchard. Now, in my class you will learn to think for yourselves again. You will learn to savor words and language because no matter what anybody tells you, words and ideas can change the world. Now I see that look in Mr. Pitts' eye, like nineteenth-century literature has nothing to do with going to business school or medical school. Right? Mr. Hopkins, you may agree with him, thinking, "Yes, we should simply study our Mr. Pritchard, and learn our rhyme and meter, and go quietly about the business of achieving other ambitions." I've a little secret for you. Huddle up. Huddle up! . . . We don't read and write poetry because it's cute. We read and write poetry because we are members of the human race, and the human race is filled with passion. Now, medicine, law, business, engineering—these are noble pursuits and necessary to sustain life. But poetry, beauty, romance, love—these are what we stay alive for. To quote from Whitman, "O me! O life! of the question of these recurring, Of the endless trains of the faithless, of cities fill'd with the foolish . . . What good amid these O me, O life? Answer: That you are here—That life exists and identity, That the powerful play goes on, and you may contribute a verse." That the powerful play goes on, and you may contribute a verse. What will your verse be?

CARPE DIEM

So mesmerizing is Keating, especially in the following encouragement, his students form a Dead Poets Society.

Keating: Seize the day. "Gather ye rosebuds while ye may." Why does the poet write these lines? Because we are food for worms, lads. Because, believe it or not, each and every one of us in this room is, one day, going to stop breathing, turn cold, and die. I would like you to step forward over here and peruse some of the faces from the past. You've walked by them many times, but I don't think you've really looked at them. They're not that different from you, are they? Same haircuts, full of hormones just like you. Invincible—just like you feel. The world is their oyster. They believe they're destined for great things, just like many of you. Their eyes are full of hope, just like you. Did they not wait until it was too late to make from their lives even one iota of what they were capable? Because you see, gentlemen, those boys are now fertilizing daffodils. But if you listen real close, you can hear them whisper their legacy to you. Go on, lean in. Listen. Do you hear it? Carpe. Hear it? Carpe. Carpe diem. Seize the day, boys. Make your lives extraordinary.

ON BEING POOR

For writer/director Preston Sturges, even the smallest role can have something pithy to say. During Sullivan's Travels, *Sullivan comes across some sound advice from, of all people . . .*

The Butler: You see, sir, rich people and theorists—who are usually rich people—think of poverty in the negative, as the lack of riches, as disease might be called the lack of health. But it isn't, sir. Poverty is not the lack of anything, but a positive plague, virulent in itself, contagious as cholera, with filth, criminality, vice and despair as only a few of its symptoms. It is to be stayed away from, even for purposes of study. It is to be shunned.

ON PRISONS

. . . And Justice For All *is a complex concept, but this hanging judge has a simple take on it.*

Judge Fleming: Prison should be a frightening place. Let those criminals create their own hellhole. Why should we help them once they're behind bars? Our job is to maintain law and order on the streets. If someone chooses to violate that law, put him away where there is no law and see how long he lasts. In fact, take away the guards. Use them only to keep the prisoners in—not to protect them from themselves. If they want to kill each other? Fine and dandy. Do you understand what I'm saying to you, for Christ's sake? Prison should be so vile and horrible that the place in itself becomes a deterrent to crime. The idea of punishment to fit the crime does not work. We need *unjust* punishment. Hang someone for armed robbery. Try it! We've got nothing to lose. The concept of rehabilitation is a farce. Do you honestly think that bringing Johnny Cash into prisons to sing railroad songs is going to rehabilitate anyone?

THE GENIUS VS. THE SHRINK

It takes a shrink to turn a math genius/delinquent into Good Will Hunting. *Will goes to a session, but he wants to avoid the tough questions. The shrink calls him on it.*

Sean: So if I asked you about art, you could give me the skinny on every art book ever written . . . Michelangelo? You know a lot about him. Life's work, political aspirations, him and the pope, sexual orientation the whole works, right? But I bet you can't tell me what it smells like in the Sistine Chapel. You've never stood there and looked up at that beautiful ceiling. Seen that . . . If I asked you about women, you'd probably give me a syllabus of your personal favorites. You may have even been laid a few times. But you can't tell me how it feels to wake up next to a woman and be truly happy. You're a tough kid. I ask you about war, and you'd probably throw Shakespeare at me, right? "Once more into the breach, dear friends." But you've never been near one. You've never held your best friend's head in your lap and watched him draw his last breath, looking to you for help. And if I asked you about love, you'd probably quote me a sonnet. But you've never looked at a woman and been totally vulnerable. Known someone could level you with her eyes. Feeling like God had put an angel on earth just for you . . . who could rescue you from the depths of hell. And you wouldn't know how it felt to be her angel and to have the love to be there for her forever. Through anything. Through cancer. You wouldn't know about sleeping sitting up in a hospital room for two months, holding her hand and not leaving because the doctors could see in your eyes that the term "visiting hours" don't apply to you. You don't know about real loss, because that only occurs when you love something more than you love yourself. I doubt you've *ever* dared to love anything that much. I look at you, I don't see an intelligent, confident man; I see a cocky, scared-shitless kid. But you're a genius, Will. No one denies that. No one could possibly understand the depths of you. But you presume to know everything about me, because you saw a painting of mine and ripped my fuckin' life apart. You're an orphan, right? Do you think I'd know the first thing about how hard your life has been, how you feel, who you are, because I read Oliver Twist? Does that encapsulate you? Personally, I don't give a shit about that, because you know what? I can't learn anything from you I can't read in some fuckin' book. Unless you wanna talk about you, who you are. And I'm fascinated. I'm in. But you don't wanna do that, do you, sport? You're terrified of what you might say. Your move, chief.

WHITE PEOPLE VS. HUMAN BEINGS

An aging Indian Chief explains to Little Big Man *the difference between the white man and their Indian tribe, known as "Human Beings."*

Old Lodge Skins: *(holding up a scalp)* Do you see this fine thing? Do you admire the humanity of it? Because the Human Beings, my son, they believe everything is alive. Not only man and animals. But also water, earth, stone. And also the things from them . . . like that hair. The man from whom this hair came, he's bald on the other side, because I now own his scalp! That is the way things are. But the white man, they believe *everything* is dead. Stone, earth, animals. And people! Even their own people! If things keep trying to live, white man will rub them out. That is the difference.

I'LL MAKE A MAN OUT OF YOU

Harold and Maude *are an unlikely romantic couple, he in his early 20s, she in her late 80s. Since most of Harold's life has been just as unorthodox as his love life (he likes to stage suicide attempts), his Uncle Victor is going to straighten him out.*

Uncle Victor: Harold, your mother has briefed me on your situation and there is no doubt in my mind of the requisite necessary action. If it was up to me, I'd process your file and ship you off to boot camp tomorrow. Your mother, however, is adamant. She does not want you in the army and insists on my holding on to your draft records. But what do you say, Harold? It's a great life. Action! Adventure! Advising. See war—firsthand! Plenty of slant-eyed girls. It will make a man out of you, Harold. You'll travel the world. Put on the uniform and take on a man's job. Walk tall—with a glint in your eye, a spring in your step, and the knowledge in your heart that you are working for peace and are serving your county. Like Nathan Hale. That's what this country needs—more Nathan Hales. And, Harold, I think I can see a little Nathan Hale in you.

MANKIND'S LEGACY

Here's a statement about man's abuse of the environment, by a marine biologist to the intrepid crew of the Starship Enterprise in 1986, as they undertake Star Trek IV: The Voyage Home.

Gillian: Since the dawn of time, men have harvested whales for a variety of purposes, most of which can be achieved synthetically at this point. One hundred years ago, using hand-thrown harpoons, man did plenty of damage—but that was nothing compared to what they've achieved in this century. This is mankind's legacy: whales hunted to the brink of extinction. Virtually gone is the blue whale, the largest creature ever to inhabit the Earth. Despite all attempts at banning whaling, there are still countries and pirates currently engaged in the slaughter of these inoffensive creatures. Where the humpback once numbered in the hundreds of thousands, today there are less than ten thousand specimens alive, and those that are taken in are no longer fully grown. In addition, many of the female whales are killed while still bearing unborn calves.

A HAPPY LIFE

Fred Astaire was Carefree *until he went to a psychiatrist. (In this context, "gay" had no sexual connotation.)*

Tony: We all try to escape reality. We all want to be something or someone entirely different. Why, when I was a kid I wanted to be a cop, then a soldier, then a fireman, then a dancer. You remember how stage struck I was. Then Dr. Von Helm psychoanalyzed me and showed me the reason. All I *thought*

I wanted was a gay life. Psychoanalysis showed me I was wrong. It's a great thing, Steve. It's the only way we can find out what we really want and why we want it.

FUCKING

Adult philosophies aside, ultimately, it's Kids *who say the darndest things.*

Telly (V.O.): When you're young, not much matters. When you find something that you care about, then that's all you got. When you're young, a lot of the time fucking is all you have, then you go to sleep at night, you dream of pussy. When you wake up, it's the same thing. It's in your face, in your dreams, you can't escape it. Sometimes when you're young, the only place to go is inside. That's just it. Fucking is what I love. Take that away from me, and I really got nothin'.

A DICK TURNS IN A TWIST

Dashiell Hammet's great pulp detective Sam Spade is about to turn Brigid, a beautiful woman, over to the police. She hasn't found the real Maltese Falcon, *so she offers herself up instead.*

Sam Spade: Listen . . . This won't do any good. You'll never understand me, but I'll try once and then give it up. Listen . . . When a man's partner is killed, he's supposed to do something about it. It doesn't make any difference what you thought of him. He was your partner and you're supposed to do something about it. Then it happens we're in the detective business. Well, when one of your organization gets killed, it's bad business to let the killer get away with it—bad all around—bad for every detective everywhere.

Brigid: You don't expect me to think that these things you're saying are sufficient reason for sending me to the . . .?

Sam Spade: Wait till I'm through. Then you can talk. Third: I've no earthly reason to think I can trust you, and if I did this and got away with it, you'd have something on me you could use whenever you wanted to. Next: since I've got something on you, I couldn't be sure you wouldn't decide to put a hole in me some day. Fifth: I wouldn't even like the idea of thinking that there might be one chance in a hundred that you'd played me for a sucker. And sixth: But that's enough. All those are on one side. Maybe some of them are unimportant. I won't argue about that. But look at the number of them. Now, on the other side we've got what? All we've got is that maybe you love me and maybe I love you.

A FATHER'S ADVICE

From Damon Runyon's unique world of Guys and Dolls *comes possibly the best advice of all.*

Sky Masterson: On the day when I left home to make my way in the world, my daddy took me to one side. "Son," my daddy says to me, "I am sorry I am not able to bankroll you to a large start, but not having the necessary lettuce to get you rolling, instead I'm going to stake you to some very valuable advice. One of these days in your travels, a guy is going to show you a brand-new deck of cards on which the seal is not yet broken. Then this guy is going to offer to bet you that he can make the jack of spades jump out of this brand-new deck of cards and squirt cider in your ear. But, son, do not accept this bet, because as sure as you stand there, you're going to wind up with an ear full of cider."

CHAPTER 2:

The Business of America

A BUSINESS FOR PRESIDENT

A perilous Stagecoach *journey features a great ensemble of passengers, including this banker, whose indignation would be more persuasive if he weren't absconding with embezzled funds.*

Gatewood: I can't get over the impertinence of that young lieutenant! I'll make it warm for that shavetail! I'll report him to Washington. We pay taxes to the government and what do we get? Not even protection from the Army. I don't know what the government's coming to! Instead of protecting businessmen, it pokes its nose into business. Hmm . . . Why, they're even talking now about having bank examiners, as if we bankers don't know how to run our own banks. I actually had a letter from some popinjay official saying they were going to inspect my books! I have a slogan, gentlemen, that should be emblazoned on every newspaper in the country: America for Americans! The government must not interfere with business! Reduce taxes! Our national debt is something shocking, over one billion dollars a year! What this country needs is a businessman for president!

A TWENTY-SEVEN-YEAR-OLD MILLIONAIRE

Stocks are sold—illegally as it turns out—to gullible investors from The Boiler Room *by means of high-pressure telemarketing sales techniques. Naturally, the business attracts young men with certain values, undoubtedly derived from the Ronald Reagan, Mike Milken era.*

Jim Young: This is the deal. I am not here to waste your time and I certainly hope you're not here to waste mine. So I'm gonna keep this short. You become an employee of this firm and you will make your first million within three years. Okay? I'm gonna repeat that. You will make a million dollars within three years of your first day of employment at JT Marlin. There is no question as to whether or not you will be a millionaire working at this firm, the only question is how many times over. You think I'm joking. I am not joking. I am a millionaire. It's a weird thing to hear, right? I'll tell you, it's a weird thing to say. I am a fucking millionaire. And guess how old I am? Twenty-seven. You know what that makes me here? A fucking senior citizen. This firm is entirely comprised of people your age, not mine. Lucky for me, I happen to be very fucking good at my job or I'd be out of one. You guys are the new blood. You're gonna go home with the kesef. You are the future big-swinging Dicks of this firm. Now, you all look money-hungry and that's good. Anybody who says money is the root of all evil doesn't have it! Money can't buy happiness? Look at the fucking smile on my face: ear to ear, baby. You want the details? I drive a Ferrari 355 Cabriolet. I have a ridiculous house on the South Fork. I have every toy you can possibly imagine. And best of all, kids, I am liquid. So, now you know what's possible, let me tell you what's required. You are required to work your fucking ass off at this firm. We want winners, not pikers. A piker walks at the bell. A piker asks how much vacation time he gets in the first year. Vacation? People come and work at this firm for one reason: to become filthy rich. That's it. We're not here to make friends. We're not saving the fucking manatees. You want vacation time? Go teach third grade public school. Okay. Your first six months at the firm are as a trainee . . . you make one hundred fifty dollars a week. After you're done training, you take the Series Seven. You pass that, you become a junior broker and you'll be opening accounts for your team leader. You open forty accounts, you start working for yourself and then . . . sky's the limit. A word about being a trainee: friends, parents, other brokers, whoever—they're gonna give you shit about it. And it's true, a hundred and fifty a week is not a lot of money, but pay no mind. You need to learn the business and this is the time to do it. Once you pass the test, none of that's gonna matter. Your friends are shit. You tell them you made twenty-five thousand last month, they're not going to believe you. Fuck them! Your parents don't like the life you lead? Fuck you, mom and dad! See how it feels when you're making their fucking Lexus payments. Now go home and think about it. Think about whether this is really for you. If you decide it isn't, listen, nothing to be embarrassed about. It's not for everyone. But if you really want this, you give me a call on Monday and we'll talk. Just don't waste my time. Okay. That's it.

ANTI-TRUST

An American crook gets a lesson on democracy from an Argentinean prosecutor, and on love from the sensuous Gilda.

Obregon: The German has been arrested. He will give us the information we want. Now, all we want from you are the patents and the agreements bearing the signatures. Let me tell you why we must know who these signers are, Mr. Farrell: so that they can be prosecuted legally for breaking the Anti-Trust laws. Restraint of trade is a crime in your country as well as many others, Mr. Farrell. Restraint is a deprivation of liberty, and I believe that word is quite prominent in your country's Declaration of Independence. Restraint is the choking-off of the natural flow, Mr. Farrell. The result is, of course, death. First the death of competition, then the death of the little man in business, then the death of conscience and decency, and finally the death of human beings at the hands of other human beings. "Trust" is a convenient but misleading word when applied to capitalistic monopoly, Mr. Farrell. "Betrayal" would be a better word. You fought in the war just passed—in the Air Force. I investigated. So it is inconceivable to me that you should share in preparing for, if not actually precipitating, another war. Since you react like a small boy, I'll explain this to you as I would to a child: If a man is hungry and a neighbor's larder is stocked with hoarded food, eventually hunger will drive that man to attack his neighbor so that he may himself survive. In other words, one man's greed and another man's need starts a fight between neighbors. A fight between nations is called a war. You're an American, Mr. Farrell—let me ask you this: Supposing the original plan of this cartel had gone through, and the control had passed into the wrong hands and another war had started? Tungsten is a strategic material. Like tin, rubber, oil, phosphates—deny any of these things to a nation at war and that nation faces defeat. For a momentary feeling of personal power, you were, in effect, declaring war on your own country and making sure of her defeat. I'm sure that isn't what you intended, Mr. Farrell. You didn't hear a word of it, did you? All you can think of is the way Gilda looked at you when you struck her, isn't it? You never intended to do that either, did you? But it was inevitable. You hit out at her just as she hit out at you tonight by making an exhibition of herself. You two kids love each other pretty terribly, don't you?

Johnny: I hate her.

Obregon: That's what I mean. It's the most curious love/hate pattern I've ever had the privilege of witnessing. And as long as you're as sick in the head as you are about her, you're not able to think about anything clearly. All right, Mr. Farrell. You are under arrest for illegally operating a gambling casino. I'm going to let you stay here under protective custody. Send for me when you can't stand it anymore. I intend to have those signatures. I can outwait you, Mr. Farrell. You see, I have the law on my side. It's a very comfortable feeling. It's something you ought to try sometime.

GOLD

Venerable character actor Walter Huston describes the Treasure of the Sierra Madre, *and what men will do to get it. (From a screenplay written by his son, screenwriter/director John Huston.)*

Howard: Gold in Mexico? Sure there is. Not ten days from here by rail and pack train, a mountain's waiting for the right guy to come along, discover her treasure, and then tickle her until she lets him have it. The question is, are you the right guy? Real bonanzas are few and far between, and they take a lot of finding. Answer me this one, will you? Why's gold worth some twenty bucks per ounce? A thousand men, say, go searching for gold. After six months, one of 'em is lucky—one out of the ten thousand. His find represents not only his own labor but that of the nine hundred ninety-nine others, to boot. Six thousand months or fifty years of scrabbling over mountains, going hungry and thirsty. An ounce of gold, mister, is worth what it is because of the human labor that went into the finding and the getting of it. There's no other explanation, mister. In itself, gold ain't good for anything much except to make jewelry and gold teeth. Gold's a devilish sort of thing, anyway. When you go out, you tell yourself, "I'll be satisfied with twenty-five thousand handsome smackers worth of it, so help me Lord and cross my heart." Fine resolution. After months of sweating yourself dizzy and growing short on provisions and finding nothing, you come down to twenty thousand and then fifteen, until finally you say, "Lord, let me find just five thousand dollars' worth and I'll never ask anything more of you the rest of my life." Here in the Oso Negro it seems like a lot. But I tell you, if you were to make a real find, you couldn't be dragged away. Not even the threat of miserable death would stop you from trying to add ten thousand more. And when you'd reach twenty-five, you'd want to make it fifty, and at fifty, a hundred—and so on. Like at roulette. . . just one more turn . . . always one more. You lose your sense of values and your character changes entirely. Your soul stops being the same as it was before. I've dug in Alaska, and in Canada and Colorado. I was in the crowd in British Honduras, where I made my boat fare back home and almost enough over to cure me of a fever I'd caught. I've dug in California and Australia . . . all over this world, practically, and I know what gold does to men's souls.

GEORGE BAILEY'S SAVINGS AND LOAN

Here's a better approach to business: George Bailey's argument for a bank with a more humanitarian bent, the Bedford Falls Savings and Loan, presented at a meeting with the arch-villain Mr. Potter and his bigwig colleagues. With businessmen like George around, It's a Wonderful Life.

George: Just a minute, just a minute. Now, hold on, Mr. Potter. You're right when you say my father was no businessman. I know that. Why he ever started this cheap, penny-ante Building and Loan, I'll never know. But neither you nor anybody else can say anything against his character, because his whole life was . . . Why, in the twenty-five years since he and Uncle Billy started this thing, he never once thought of himself. Isn't that right, Uncle Billy? He didn't save enough money to send Harry to school, let alone me. But he did help a few people get out of your slums, Mr. Potter. And what's wrong with that? Why . . . here, you're all businessmen here. Doesn't it make them better citizens? Doesn't it make them better customers? You, you said, what'd you say just a minute ago? They had to wait and save their money before they even ought to think of a decent home. Wait! Wait for what? Until their children grow up and leave them? Until they're so old and broken-down that they . . . Do you know how long it takes a working man to save five thousand dollars? Just remember this, Mr. Potter, that this rabble you're talking about . . . they do most of the working and paying and living and dying in this community. Well, is it too much to have them work and pay and live and die in a couple of decent rooms and a bath? Anyway, my father didn't think so. People were human beings to him, but to you, a warped, frustrated old man, they're cattle. Well, in my book he died a much richer man than you'll ever be. You're talking about something you can't get your fingers on, and it's galling you. That's what you're talking about, I know. Well, I've said too much. I . . . you're the Board here. You do what you want with this thing. Just one thing more, though. This town needs this measly one-horse institution, if only to have some place where people can come without crawling to Potter. Come on, Uncle Billy!

ENTITLEMENT PROGRAMS

John Wayne hears of the government's plans for programs like unemployment and social security. His response is Without Reservations.

Rusty Thomas: Have you ever heard of some fellas who first came to this country? You know what they found? The found a howling wilderness. With summers too hot and winters freezing. And they also found some unpleasant little characters who painted their faces. Do you think these pioneers filled out form number X2677 and sent in a report saying the Indians were a little unreasonable? Did they have insurance for their old age? For their crops, for their houses? They did not. They looked at the land and the forests and the rivers. They looked at their wives, and their kids and their houses. They looked up at the sky and they said, "Thanks, God. We'll take it from here."

CHAPTER 3:

Characters

VENGEANCE

A Gladiator *makes a promise.*

Maximus: I am Maximus Decimus Meridas, Commander of the Army of the North, General of the Western Armies, loyal servant to the true emperor, Marcus Aurelius. Father to a murdered son. Husband to a murdered wife. And I shall have my vengeance, in this life or the next.

IT'S A LOUSY JOB

When bad guys arrive at High Noon, *it calls for the sheriff to provide an honest description of his life.*

Howe: It's a rotten life. You risk your skin catching killers and the juries let them go so they can come back and shoot at you again. If you're honest, you're poor your whole life, and in the end you wind up dying all alone in a dirty street, or some stinking alley. For what? For nothing. A tin star.

BUT SOMEBODY HAS TO DO IT

In a meeting of the townspeople, one man advises discretion as the better part of valor, proposing that the sheriff leave town sooner rather than later.

Jonas Anderson: All right, I'll say this: what this town owes Will Kane here can never be paid with money, and don't ever forget it. He's the best marshal we ever had, maybe the best marshal we'll ever have. So if Miller comes back here today, it's our problem, not his. It's our problem because this is our town. We made it with our own hands out of nothing, and if we want to keep it decent, keep it growing, we gotta think mighty clear here today. And we gotta have the courage to do what we think is right! No matter how hard it is. All right. There's gonna be fighting when Kane and Miller meet. And somebody's gonna get hurt, that's for sure. Now, people up North are thinking about this town—thinking mighty hard, thinking about sending money down here to put up stores and to building factories. It'll mean a lot to this town, an awful lot. But if they're gonna read about shooting and killing in the streets, what are they gonna think then? I'll tell ya: They're going to think this is just another wide-open town. And everything we worked for will be wiped out. In one day, this town will be set back five years. And I don't think we can let that happen. Mind you, you all know how I feel about this man. He's a mighty brave man. A good man. He didn't have to come back here today, and for his sake and the sake of this town I wish he hadn't. Because if he's not here when Miller comes, my hunch is there won't be any trouble. Not one bit. Tomorrow we'll have a new marshal, and if we can all agree here to offer him our services, I think we can handle anything that comes along. To me that makes sense. To me that's the only way out of this. Will, I think you better go while there's still time. It's better for you and it's better for us.

THE POLICE OFFICER

Things haven't changed much in The Asphalt Jungle, *but the pay is better.*

Hardy: Let me put it this way: It's nothing strange that there are corrupt officers in the police department. There would have to be. People are people, even in blue uniform. The dirt they are trying to clean up is bound to soil them a little. They can become brutal, grafting, weak, inefficient. But not all of them. Not one in ten, nor one in a hundred. The ordinary patrolman is an honest man doing an honest job. Look here—(*he turns on a police radio*) Listen—I know you're police reporters, and you hear this all day long. But I want you to listen with your conscience—not just your ears. We send police assistance to every one of these calls. Because they're not just code numbers on a radio beam. They're cries for help; people are being cheated—robbed, murdered, raped—every day in the year. And that's not exceptional, that's usual. And it's the same in every city in the modern world. But suppose we had no police force—good or bad. Suppose we had — (turns it off) just silence. No one to listen. No one to answer. The war is finished. The jungle wins. The criminals take over. Think about it. Well, gentlemen. Three men are in jail—three dead, one by his own hand, and one man is a fugitive and, we've reason to think, badly wounded. Six out of seven, that's not bad. But we'll get the last one, too. In many ways he's the most dangerous of them all. A hardened killer, a hooligan, a man without human feeling or human mercy.

LITTLE GEORGIE COHAN

Before he was a Yankee Doodle Dandy, *George M. Cohan was a cocky little kid. Even his father knew it. When little Georgie lands the title role in* Peck's Bad Boy, *he discovers that the neighborhood kids can't separate fact from fiction, and they beat him up.*

Jerry: The way I look at it, it's a fine tribute to Georgie's acting. The way he plays it, every tough kid in America will want to take a punch at Peck's Bad Boy, just to see what happens.

George: *What!* Have I got to go through this *every* night?

Jerry: And matinees, Wednesday, and Saturday. Georgie—those boys did you a great favor—and they saved me some trouble. Most actors give their whole lives to their profession without once scoring a hit. You're lucky; you're a hit at the age of thirteen. You're going to be a big star, there's no doubt about that. You're going to be surrounded by a lot of admirers and backslappers—but you're going to have very few friends. The way you treated your fellow actors a little while ago will take care of that. Those kids in the street gave you a good idea of what a performer means to the public. What friends—real friends—mean to a performer, you'll have to find out for yourself. I've been in this profession a long time but I never ran across a performer who, in the long run, wouldn't rather be a great guy than a great actor. That is—until I made your acquaintance.

A PUBLISHER'S CREED

Citizen Kane *has a dual identity, and he knows it.*

Kane: The trouble is, Mr. Thatcher, you don't realize you're talking to two people. As Charles Foster Kane, who has eighty-two thousand, six hundred and thirty-one shares of Metropolitan Transfer—you see, I do have a rough idea of my holdings—I sympathize with you. Charles Foster Kane is a dangerous scoundrel; his paper should be run out of town and a committee should be formed to boycott him. You may, if you can form such a committee, put me down for a contribution of one thousand dollars. On the other hand—I am the publisher of the Enquirer. As such, it is my duty—I'll let you in on a little secret, it is also my pleasure—to see to it that decent, hard-working people of this city are not robbed blind by a group of money-mad pirates because, God help them, they have no one to look after their interests! I'll let you in on another little secret, Mr. Thatcher: I think I'm the man to do it. You see, I have money and property. If I don't defend the interests of the underprivileged, somebody else will—maybe somebody without any money or any property. And that would be too bad. But you're right—we did lose a million dollars last year. We expect to lose a million next year, too. You know, Mr. Thatcher, at the rate of a million a year, we'll have to close this place in sixty years.

CHANGING TIMES

The only man who can tell him the truth doesn't always buy into the eccentric Kane philosophy.

Leland: You talk about the people as though they belong to you. As long as I can remember, you've talked about giving the people their rights as though you could make them a present of liberty—in reward for services rendered. You remember the working man? You used to write an awful lot about the working man. Well, he's turning into something called organized labor, and you're not going to like that a bit when you find out it means that he thinks he's entitled to something as his right, and not your gift. And listen, Charles: When your precious underprivileged really do get together—that's going to add up to something bigger than your privilege—and then I don't know what you'll do. Sail away to a desert island, probably, and lord it over the monkeys.

THE JOHN DOES

Of all the champions of the little people, screenwriter Robert Riskin stands tallest. In this speech, he asks us to Meet John Doe.

John: Ladies and gentlemen: I am the man you all know as John Doe. I took that name because it seems to describe—because it seems to describe the average man, and that's me. *And that's me.* Well, it *was* me—before I said I was gonna jump off the City Hall roof at midnight on Christmas Eve. Now I'd guess I'm not average any more. Now I'm getting all sorts of attention, from big shots, too. The mayor and the governor, for instance. They don't like those articles I've been writing. Well, people like the governor—people like the governor and that fella there can—can stop worrying. I'm not gonna talk about them. I'm gonna talk about us, the average guys, the John Does. If anybody should ask you what the average John Doe is like, they couldn't tell him because he's a million and one things. He's Mr. Big and Mr. Small. He's simple and he's wise. He's inherently honest, but he's got a streak of larceny in his heart. He seldom walks up to a public telephone without shoving his finger into the slot to see if somebody left a nickel there. He's the man the ads are written for. He's the fella everybody sells things to. He's Joe Doakes, the world's greatest stooge and the world's greatest strength. Yes, sir. Yessir, we're a great family, the John Does. We're the meek who are, who are supposed to inherit the earth. You'll find us everywhere. We raise the crops, we dig the mines, work the factories, keep the books, fly the planes and drive the busses! And when a cop yells: "Stand back there, you!" he means us, the John Does. We've existed since time began. We built the pyramids, we saw Christ crucified, pulled the oars for Roman emperors, sailed the boats for Columbus, retreated from Moscow with Napoleon, and froze with Washington at Valley Forge! Yes, sir. We've been in there dodging left hooks since before history began to walk! In our struggle for freedom we've hit the canvas many a time, but we always bounced back! Because we're the *people*—and we're tough! They've started a lot of talk about free people going soft—that we can't take it. That's a lot of hooey! A free people can beat the world at anything, from war to tiddly winks, if we all pull in the same direction! I know a lot of you are saying, "What can I do? I'm just a little punk. I don't count." Well, you're dead wrong! The little punks have always counted because, in the long run, the character of a country is the sum total of the character of its little punks. But we've all got to get in there and pitch! We can't win the old ball game unless we have teamwork. And that's where every John Doe comes in. It's up to him to get together with his teammate! And your teammates, my friends, is the guy next door to you. Your neighbor! He's a terribly important guy, that guy next door! You're gonna need him and he's gonna need you, so look him up! If he's sick, call on him! If he's hungry, feed him! If he's out of a job, find him one! To most of you, your neighbor is a stranger, a guy with a barking dog and a high fence around him. Now, you can't be a stranger to any guy that's on your own team. So tear down the fence that separates you, tear down the fence and you'll tear down a lot of hates and prejudices! Tear down all the fences in the country and you'll really have teamwork! I know a lot of you are saying to yourselves: "He's asking for a miracle to happen. He's expecting people to change, all of a sudden." Well, you're wrong. It's no miracle. It's no miracle because it happens once every year. And so do you. At Christmas time! There's something swell about the spirit of Christmas, to see what it does to people, all kinds of people . . . Now, why can't that spirit, that same warm Christmas spirit last the whole year round? Gosh, if it ever did, if each and every John Doe would make that spirit last three hundred sixty-five days out of the year, we'd develop such a strength, we'd create such a tidal wave of good will, that no human force could stand against it. Yes sir, my friends, the meek can only inherit the earth when the John Does start loving their neighbors. You'd better start right now. Don't wait till the game is called on account of darkness! Wake up, John Doe! You're the hope of the world!

EVOLUTION OF THE JEWISH MERCHANT

Sol Nazerman, survivor of the Auschwitz concentration camp, now runs a pawnshop in Spanish Harlem. A young Puerto Rican asks him, "How come you people come to business so naturally?" The Pawnbroker explains.

Sol: You begin with several thousand years during which you have nothing except a great bearded legend. Nothing else. You have no land to grow food on. No land on which to hunt. Not enough time in one place to have a geography, or an army, or a land-myth. You have only a little brain in your head and this bearded legend to sustain you, convince you there is something special about you, even in your poverty. But this little brain . . . that is the real key. With it, you obtain a small piece of cloth and you cut it in two, and sell the two pieces for a penny or two more than you paid for the one. With this money, then, you buy a slightly larger piece of cloth. Which perhaps may be cut into three pieces. And sold for three pennies profit. You must never succumb to buying an extra piece of bread at this point. Or a toy for your child. Immediately, you must go out and buy a still larger cloth, or two large cloths. And repeat the process. And so you continue until there is no longer any temptation to dig in the earth and grow food. No longer any desire to gaze at limitless land which is in your name. You repeat this process over and over for centuries and centuries. And then, all of a sudden, you discover you have a mercantile heritage. You are known as a merchant. You're also known as a man with secret resources, usurer, pawnbroker, a witch, or what have you. But by the end, it is instinct. Do you understand?

MY FACE

A Grand Duchess wakes up in the morning, looks in her mirror, and doesn't like what she sees.

Swana: It's really a wretched morning . . . wretched. I can't get myself right. I wanted to look mellow, and I look brittle. My face doesn't compose well . . . all highlights . . . how can I dim myself down, Leon? Suggest something. I am so bored with this face. I wish I had someone else's face. Whose face would you have if you had your choice? Oh, well, I guess one gets the face one deserves.

I AM GOD

An investigation into a surgical case brings forth the arrogance and Malice *of a doctor.*

Jed: No, no. Let them address me. It's about time I got to answer some questions here. The question is, "Do I have a God complex?" Dr. Kessler says, yes. Which makes me wonder if this . . . lawyer has any idea as to the kind of grades one must receive in college to be accepted to medical school? Or if you have the vaguest clue about how talented someone must be to lead a surgical team? I have an M.D. from Harvard. I am boardcertified in cardiothoracic medicine and trauma surgery. I have been awarded citations from seven different medical journals in New England, and I am never, ever sick at sea. So I ask you: When someone goes into that chapel, and they fall on their knees and they pray to God that their wife doesn't miscarry, or that their daughter doesn't bleed to death, or that their mother doesn't suffer acute neural trauma from postoperative shock, who do you think they're praying to? Now, you go ahead and read your bible—Dennis—and you go to church, and with any luck you might even win the annual raffle. But if you're looking for God, why, he was in operating room number two, on November 17, and he doesn't like being second-guessed. You want to know if I have a God complex? Let me tell you something—I AM GOD, and this sideshow is over.

THREE LEGENDS OF DRACULA

On the trail of Dracula...

Van Helsing: Senor Harker, I have devoted my life to the study of the strangest things. To little known facts that maybe the world had better ignore. But I quietly accept vulgar things. Dracula's name is associated to a legend that is still told among Dracula's fellow countrymen. This legend alludes to an old family that disappeared about five centuries ago and was supposed to be formed by vampires. As I discovered by chance that Dracula was not reflected in the mirror; and, besides, that three big boxes had been sent to Carfax Abbey; and I also knew that a vampire must sleep during the day in his native land, I understood at once that Dracula had to be the person who Renfield calls "Master," a being who is not dead and has been able to prolong his life beyond the natural limits, feeding himself on the blood of other living creatures. We can only save Eva if we find the place where the living corpse of the vampire rests and we drive a stake through his heart.

More on the famous Count...

Van Helsing: The vampire bat must consume ten times its own weight in fresh blood each day or its own blood cells will die. Cute little vermin, *Ja?* Blood and the diseases of the blood, such as syphilis, will concern us here. The very name "venereal diseases," the "diseases of Venus," imputes to them divine origin. They are involved in that sex problem about which the ethics and ideals of Christian civilization are concerned. In fact, civilization and syphilization have advanced together.

Furthermore . . .

Van Helsing: Vampires do exist. This one we fight, this one we face, has the strength of twenty people, and you can testify to that, Mr. Harker. He can command the meaner things: the bat . . . the rodent . . . the wolf . . . and all the elements. He can come in mist and vapor and fog, and vanish at will. He can do all these things, yet, he, this Dracula . . . can be killed.

I AM AN ALCOHOLIC

How one becomes an alcoholic is described by this one, a life that is more than
The Lost Weekend.

Don: It shrinks my liver, doesn't it, Nat? It pickles my kidneys. Yes. But
what does it do to my mind? It tosses the sandbags overboard so the balloon
can soar. Suddenly, I'm above the ordinary. I'm competent, supremely
competent. I'm walking a tightrope over Niagara Falls. I'm one of the
great ones. I'm Michelangelo molding the beard of Moses. I'm Van Gogh,
painting pure sunlight. I'm Horowitz, playing the Emperor Concerto.
I'm John Barrymore before the movies got him by the throat. I'm Jesse
James and his two brothers, all three of them. I'm W. Shakespeare. And
out there it's not Third Avenue any longer. It's the Nile, Nat. The Nile, and
down it moves the barge of Cleopatra. Come here. Purple the sails, and so
perfumed that the winds were lovesick with them; the oars were silver,
which to the tune of flutes kept stroke . . . A writer. Silly, isn't it? You know,
in college I passed for a genius. They couldn't get out the college magazine
without one of my stories. Boy, was I hot, Hemingway stuff. I reached my
peak when I was nineteen. Sold a piece to the Atlantic Monthly. Reprinted
in the Readers Digest. Who wants to stay in college when he's Hemingway?
My mother bought me a brand-new typewriter, and I moved right in on
New York. Well, the first thing I wrote, that didn't quite come off. And
the second, I dropped. The public wasn't ready for that one. I started
a third and a fourth . . . only by then, somebody began to look over my
shoulder and whisper, in a thin, clear voice like the E-string on a violin.
Don Birnam, he'd whisper, it's not good enough. Not that way. How about
a couple of drinks just to set it on its feet, huh? So I had a couple. Oh,
what a great idea that was. That made all the difference. Suddenly I could
see the whole thing . . . the tragic sweep of the great novel, beautifully
proportioned. But before I could really grab it and throw it down on paper,
the drinks would wear off and everything would be gone, like a mirage.
Then there was despair, and a drink to counterbalance despair, and one to
counterbalance the counterbalance. And I'd sit in front of that typewriter,
trying to squeeze out one page that was halfway decent, and that guy would
pop up again.

Helen: What guy? Who are you talking about?

Don: The other Don Birnam. There are two of us, you know: Don the drunk and Don the writer. And the drunk would say to the writer, come on, you idiot. Let's get some good out of that portable. Let's hock it. Let's take it to that pawn shop over on Third Avenue, it's always good for ten dollars, another drink, another binge, another bender and a spree. Such humorous words. I tried to break away from that guy a lot of times, but no good. You know once I even got myself a gun and some bullets. I was gonna do it on my thirtieth birthday. Here are the bullets. The gun went for three quarts of whiskey. That other Don wanted us to have a drink first. He always wants us to have a drink first. The flop suicide of a flop writer.

DR. EVIL'S HERITAGE

Comic actor Mike Myers played both Austin Powers *and Austin's arch-nemesis, Dr. Evil, to whom he gave an interesting back-story.*

Dr. Evil: Very well, where do I begin? My father was a relentlessly self-improving boulangerie owner from Belgium with low-grade narcolepsy and a penchant for buggery. My mother was a fifteen-year-old French prostitute named Chloe, with webbed feet. My father would womanize, he would drink, he would make outrageous claims like he invented the question mark. Sometimes he would accuse chestnuts of being lazy, the sort of general malaise that only the genius possess and the insane lament. My childhood was typical, summers in Rangoon, luge lessons. In the spring we'd make meat helmets. When I was insolent I was placed in a burlap bag and beaten with reeds, pretty standard really. At the age of twelve I received my first scribe. At the age of fourteen a Zoroastrian woman named Vilma ritualistically shaved my testicles. There really is nothing like a shorn scrotum—it's breathtaking. I suggest you try it.

LAWYERS

Respect for lawyers is rapidly diminishing in a litigious world. Especially in Philadelphia. *(Although this speech from an early draft didn't make it into the film, I couldn't resist its sentiments.)*

Judge Garnett: I've asked the litigants to be present for this conference, in the hope we can settle this matter today, among ourselves . . . There is nothing I hate more than to see lawyers suing each other. If you look at the opinion polls, when Mr. John Q. Citizen is asked to rank professions according to the respect he holds for them . . . Where are the lawyers? Somewhere below personal fitness trainers and only slightly above child pornographers. If we keep suing each other, if we fail to settle the smallest difference among ourselves with mutual respect, if we continue to scrap like bucks in heat, we'll fall lower on that list. And when people lose respect for lawyers, they lose respect for the law. And when this society

loses all respect for the law, we'll be murdered in our beds, my friends, our cherished institutions will be burned to the ground and our children and our grandchildren will live like savages.

COMMUNISTS

In May of 1980, Fidel Castro allowed 125,000 people to leave Cuba for the United States. One of them became Scarface, *but if you were an I.N.S. officer, you might buy this spiel too.*

Tony: Hey, so I fuck Castro? What's it to you? You a communist or something? How would you like it they tell you all the time what to think, what to do; you wanna be like a sheep, like everybody else? Baa, Baa? Puta! You want a stoolie on every block? You wanna work eight hours a day and you never own nothing? I ate octopus three times a day, fucking octopus is coming out of my ears, fuckin' Russian shoes are eating through my feet. Whaddaya want? You want me to stay there? Hey, I'm no little whore, I'm no stinking thief! I'm Tony Montana and I'm a political prisoner here from Cuba, and I want my fucking "Human Rights," just like President Jimmy Carter says, okay?

HEROES OF THE UNIVERSE

Movie schizophrenics come in many guises. The doctor who treats Lilith *almost admires them.*

Dr. Lavrier: Some of these people have such extraordinary minds, such extraordinary sensibilities. Too extraordinary, I think, sometimes. This is all just scientific theory . . . maybe it's romantic . . . but I often compare them to fine crystal which has been shattered by the shock of some intolerable revelation. I often had a feeling when I talked with them that they had seen too much with too fine an instrument. They had been close to some extreme, something absolute, and then blasted by it. As though they'd been destroyed, one might say, by their own excellence. Regarded in this way, they are the heroes of the universe, its finest product and its noblest casualty. Schizophrenia, however, is far from being an exclusive affliction of superior minds. As a matter of fact, by using a substance from the blood of humans, schizophrenia has been induced in dogs, spiders, as well as men. As you will note, the webs of most "normal" spider species are as distinctive and invariable as their coloring. But the "mad" ones spin out fantastic, asymmetrical, and rather nightmarish designs. A most unsettling fact.

TRANSVESTITES

Ed Wood, famous more for the Tim Burton movie about him than for directing his own ultra-low budget films, was perhaps ahead of his time with the transvestite flick, Glen or Glenda? *Here the narrator introduces us to the peculiar characteristics of our hero. Or is that heroine?*

Narrator: Are we sure? Nature makes mistakes, it's proven everyday. This person is a transvestite—a man who is more comfortable wearing women's clothing. The term transvestite is the name given by medical science to those persons who wear the clothing of the opposite sex. The title of this can only be labeled "Behind Locked Doors." Give this man satin undies, a dress, a sweater and a skirt, or even the lounging outfit he has on, and he's the happiest individual in the world. He can work better, think better, he can play better, and he can be more of a credit to his community and his government because he is happy. These things are his comfort. But why the wig and makeup? He dares to enter the street dressed in the clothes he so much desires to wear. But only if he really appears female. The long hair, the makeup, the clothing, the actual contours of a girl. Most transvestites do not want to change their life, their bodies; many of them simply want to change the clothing they wear to that as worn by the opposite sex. Glen is engaged to be married to Barbara, a lovely, intelligent girl.

Moreover . . .

Narrator: Modern man is a hard-working human. Throughout the day his mind and his muscles are busy at building the modern world and its business administration. His clothing is rough, coarse, starched, according to the specifications of his accepted job. At home, what does man have to look forward to for his body comfort? The things provided for his home. A wool or flannel robe, his feet encased in the same thick, tight-fitting leather that his shoes are made of . . . these are the things provided for his home comfort. It doesn't look so comfortable, does it? And get the hat—or better still, get the receding hairline. Men's hats are so tight they cut off the blood flow to the head, thus cutting off the growth of hair. Seven out of ten men wear a hat, so the advertisements say. Seven out of ten men are bald. But what about the ladies? Yes, modern woman is a hard-working individual also. But when modern woman's day of work is done, that which is designed for her comfort *is* comfort. Hats that give no obstruction to the blood flow, hats that do not crush the hair. Interesting thought, isn't it? Just for comparison, let's go native. Back to the animal instinct. There, in the lesser civilized part of the world, it's the male who adorns himself with the fancy objects, such as paints, frills, and masks. The true instinct. The animal instinct. Bird and animal life. Is it not so that it's the male who is the fancy one? Could it be that the male was meant to attract the attention of the female? What's so wrong about that? Where is the animal instinct in modern civilization? Female has the fluff and the finery, as specified by those who design and sell. Little Miss Female, you should feel quite proud of the situation. You, of course, realize it's predominantly men who design your clothes, your jewelry, your makeup, your hair styling, your perfume. But life, even thought its changes are slow, moves on. There's no law against wearing such apparel on the street, as long as it can be distinguished that man is man and woman is woman. But, what is it that would happen were this individual to appear on the street? You're doing it now—laughing. Yet, it's not a situation to be laughed at. Thus, the strange case of Glen, who was Glenda, one and the same person. Not half man-half woman but, nevertheless, man and woman in the same body, even though by all outward appearances Glen is fully and completely a man.

A DUAL PERSONALITY

Norman Bates, owner/operator of the Bates motel, where pretty girls check in but they don't check out, is Psycho. *Here's why.*

Dr. Richmond: Like I said—the mother . . . Now, to understand it the way I understood it, hearing it from the mother—that is, from the mother half of Norman's mind—you have to go back ten years, to the time when Norman murdered his mother and her lover. Now, he was already dangerously disturbed—had been ever since his father died. His mother was a clinging, demanding woman, and for years the two of them lived as if there was no one else in the world. Then she met a man—and it seemed to Norman that she threw him over for this man. Now, that pushed him over the line and he killed them both. Matricide is probably the most unbearable crime of all—most unbearable to the son who commits it. So he had to erase the crime, at least in his own mind. He stole her corpse. A weighted coffin was buried. He hid the body in the fruit cellar. Even treated it to keep it as well as it would keep. And that still wasn't enough. She was there but she was a corpse. So he began to think and speak for her—give her half his life, so to speak. At times he could be both personalities, carry on conversations. At other times the mother half took over completely. Now, he was never all Norman but he was often only Mother. And because he was so pathologically jealous of her, he assumed that she was as jealous of him. Therefore, if he felt a strong attraction to any other woman, the Mother side of him would go wild. When he met your sister, he was touched by her, aroused by her. He wanted her. That set off the jealous mother, and Mother killed the girl. Now, after the murder Norman returned as if from a deep sleep. And, like a dutiful son, covered up all traces of the crime he was convinced his mother had committed.

A MOTHER TURNS IN HER SON

But "Mother" lets the blame fall on "Norman."

Mother: It's sad when a mother has to speak the words that condemn her own son. I couldn't allow them to believe that I would commit murder. They'll put him away now, as I should have, years ago. He was always bad, and in the end he intended to tell them I killed those girls and that man. As if I could do anything except just sit and stare, like one of his stuffed birds. Oh, they know I can't even move a finger, and I won't. I'll just sit here and be quiet, just in case they do suspect me. They're probably watching me. Well, let them. Let them see what kind of a person I am. I'm not even gonna swat that fly. I hope they are watching. They'll see. They'll see and they'll know, and they'll say, "Why, she wouldn't even harm a fly."

A PEDOPHILE'S CONFESSION

Child-murderers give even career criminals a bad name, so when one stalks the city of Berlin, the underground criminal class sets out to find him. They succeed, and, in one if the most memorable scenes in the early talkie titled just M, *the trapped psychotic killer of children confesses.*

Hans Breckert: What do you know about it? Who are you anyway? Who are you? Criminals. Are you proud of yourselves? Proud of breaking safes or cheating at cards, things you can just as well keep your fingers off. You wouldn't need to do all that if you'd learn a proper trade. Or if you'd work, but if you weren't a bunch of lazy bastards . . . but I . . .I can't help myself—I have no control over this. This evil thing inside me, the fire, the voices, the torment! It's there all the time—driving me to wander the streets, following me silently. But I can feel it there—it's me, pursuing myself—I want to escape, to escape from myself but it's impossible . . . I can't escape, I have to obey it, I have to run endless streets—I want to escape, to get away, and I'm pursued by ghosts—ghosts of mothers and of those children, they never leave me, they are there, always there, always, always except when I do it—when I . . . then I can't remember anything and afterwards I see those posters and read what I've done. Did I do that? But I can't remember anything about it, but who will believe me? Who knows what it's like to be me? How I'm forced to act—how I must—must—don't want to—but must—and then a voice screams—I can't bear to hear it—I can't go on, I can't go on . . .

ALVY'S INTROSPECTION

The redoubtable Woody Allen often finds time in his films for a fair amount of introspection. Here's Woody—excuse me, Annie Hall's boyfriend, Alvy—describing his personal angst.

Alvy: There's an old joke: Uh, two elderly women are at a Catskill Mountain resort, and one of 'em says, "Boy, the food at this place is really terrible." The other one says, "Yeah, I know, and such . . . small portions." Well, that's essentially how I feel about life. Full of loneliness and misery and suffering and unhappiness, and it's all over much too quickly. The . . . the other important joke for me is one that's, uh, usually attributed to Groucho Marx, but I think it appears originally in Freud's *"Wit and Its Relation to the Unconscious."* And it goes like this—I'm paraphrasing—Uh . . . "I would never wanna belong to any club that would have someone like me for a member." That's the key joke of my adult life in terms of my relationships with women. Tsch, you know, lately the strangest things have been going through my mind, 'cause I turned forty, tsch, and I guess I'm going through a life crisis or something, I don't know, and I, uh . . . and I'm not worried about aging. I'm not one of those characters, you know. Although I'm balding slightly on top, that's the worst you can say about me. I, uh, I think I'm going to get better as I get older, you know? I think I'm gonna be the . . . the balding, virile type, you know, as opposed to say, the, uh, distinguished gray, for instance, you know? 'Less I'm neither of those two. Unless I'm one of those guys with saliva dribbling out of his mouth who wanders into a cafeteria with a shopping bag, screaming about socialism. (*Sighs*) Annie and I broke up and I—I still can't get my mind around that. You know, I—I keep sifting the pieces o' the relationship through my mind and—and examining my life and tryin' to figure out where did the screwup come, you know. And a year ago we were . . . Tsch, in love. You know, and, and, and . . . And it's funny, I'm not—I'm not a morose type. I'm not a depressive character. I, I, I uh, (*laughs*) you know, I was a reasonably happy kid, I guess. I was brought up in Brooklyn during World War Two . . .

CHAPTER 4:

Places

THE MOST ROMANTIC CITY IN THE WORLD

Some cities have real character. This one is described by An American in Paris.

Jerry: This is Paris, and I'm an American who lives here. My name is Jerry Mulligan; I'm an ex-G.I. When the government decided they could fight the peace without me, I stayed on. And, I can tell you, I wouldn't leave for anything in the world. Paris is an amazing and fascinating city. And yet, if you asked me why it is so, I couldn't give you a logical answer. It isn't the Champs Elysees. That's where we are now. Or the splendor of the Place de la Concorde. Or the sun dancing on the gardens of the Tuilleries. Or the treasures of the Louvre. Or the gothic glory of Notre Dame. No, you can't define Paris with such inferior stuff as logic, Paris is a mood, a taste, a longing you didn't know you had until it was answered. I guess it's like love, or art, or faith. It can't be explained, only felt.

But even the City of Lights can't mend a broken heart.

Jerry: Paris! Not this city! It's too real and too beautiful. It never lets you forget a thing. It reaches in and opens you wide, and you stay that way. I came to Paris to study and to paint it because Utrillo did, and Lautrec did, and Rouault did, and I loved what they created, and I thought that something would happen to me, too. Well, it happened all right! Maybe that's enough for some but it isn't anymore for me. The more beautiful everything is—the more it will hurt without you.

PIG ALLEY

Another view of Paris, this one as a Battleground.

Holley: Paris? Well, of course I spent all my spare time in the art galleries, but I happened to hear about a place might interest you. Pig Alley! Be sure to take your dog tags with you, because one night in Pig Alley and you're gonna think you're the Caliph of Baghdad. You guys talk about Piccadilly Circus. Compared to Pig Alley, that's like the quiet room in a limey YMCA. You can't miss there!—I'm tellin' ya, you can't miss! All you need is a class A uniform and about six month's pay, and where else are you gonna make a better investment? The MP's have had more casualties in Pig Alley than in the rest of the ETO. They got a problem with MP's in Paris, no kiddin'. Half of them are in the hospital and the rest are volunteering for the paratroops.

THE WICKEDEST CITY IN THE WORLD

San Francisco *has a different flavor.*

Mrs. Burley: They call us the wickedest city in the world. And it's true! The whole town's rotten! And it's a bitter shame—it is—for deep down underneath all our evil and sin we've got right here in San Francisco *the greatest set of human bein's ever rounded up in one spot!* Sure—they had to have *wild adventure* in their *hearts* and *dynamite* in their blood to start out for here in the first place. And they had to laugh at death and danger the whole way—in order to get through! That's why they're so full of untamed deviltry today. But we mustn't go on like we're doin'—blasphemous and sinful, and with no feelin' for God in our hearts.

BRIDGEPORT VS. NEW YORK

Bringing Up Baby isn't a sequel to Father of the Bride—*Baby is a leopard. Paleontologist Cary Grant knows a thing or two about where he and Katharine Hepburn ought to live.*

David: Now, Bridgeport is a nice little town, but with a population of fifty thousand you can't expect gaiety. New York, on the other hand, with seven million people, naturally tends to have centers of entertainment. All the best talent quite reasonably flows to a point where there will be more people to appreciate it.

AFRICA

The cradle of civilization? Out of Africa.

Karen: I had a farm in Africa at the foot of the Ngong hills. The equator runs across the highlands, a hundred miles to the north, and the farm lay at an altitude of over six thousand feet. In the daytime you felt that you had got high up, near to the sun, but the early mornings and evenings were limpid and restful, and the nights were cold. The geographical position and the height of the land combined to create a landscape that had not its like in all the world. There was no fat in it, and no luxuriance anywhere; it was Africa, distilled up through six thousand feet, like the strong and refined essence of a continent. The colors were dry and burnt, like the colors in pottery. Upon the grass of the great plains the crooked bare old thorn-trees were scattered, and the grass was spiced like thyme and bog-myrtle; in some places the scent was so strong that it smarted in the nostrils. The views were immensely wide. Everything that you saw made for greatness and freedom and unequaled nobility. In the middle of the day the air was alive over the land like a flame burning; it scintillated, waved, and shone like running water, mirrored and doubled all objects, and created great Fata Morgana. Up in this high air, you breathed easily, drawing in a vital assurance and lightness of heart. In the highlands, you woke up in the morning and thought: Here I am. Where I ought to be.

CHAPTER 5

War and Peace

On the Frontier

WHAT COURAGE IS

You don't have to carry a gun to be courageous, as one of The Magnificent Seven *explains here.*

Village Boy: We're ashamed to live here. Our fathers are cowards.

Bernardo O'Reilly: Don't you ever say that again about your fathers, because they are not cowards. You think I am brave because I carry a gun. Well, your fathers are much braver because they carry responsibility—for you, your brothers, your sisters, and your mothers. And this responsibility is like a big rock that weighs a ton. It bends and it twists them, until finally it buries them under the ground. And there's nobody says they have to do this. They do it because they love you, and because they want to. I have never had this kind of courage. Running a farm, working like a mule every day with no guarantee anything will ever come of it . . . this is bravery.

World War I

TO A DEAD SOLDIER

Here's a view of war from the trenches, where, temporarily, it's All Quiet on the Western Front. *After killing a man, this soldier, is unable to tear himself away from his lifeless foe, initiates a conversation with the corpse.*

Paul: You know I can't run away, that's why you accuse me! I tell you, I didn't want to kill you! I tried to keep you alive! If you jumped in here again, I wouldn't do it. You see—when you jumped in here, you were my enemy—I thought of your hand-grenades, of your bayonet, of your rifle—and I was afraid of you! But you're just a man like me—and I killed you. Forgive me, comrade. If you have just a little breath left, say that for me—say you forgive me! No, no, you're dead! You can't tell me that! Dead! If you had only run two yards further to the left, I wouldn't have killed you—

you'd be alive now. Why don't they teach us in training school that you're just poor devils like us. And you are just as anxious for you, and you have the same fear of death and the same dying and the same agony! Only you're better off than I am—you're through—they can't do any more to you, now. You're better off—I've got to go on and kill or be killed. And if I die, I'll have to die the way you did—and if I live, I'll have to remember the way you died—and you'll follow me and I'll have to think about you—because it was me that killed you! Oh, God! Why did they do this to us? We only wanted to live—you and I—why should they send us out to fight each other? Why should we be left all alone here—all alone with death? How could you be my enemy? If we threw away these rifles and these uniforms, you could be my brother, just like Kat and Albert. Take twenty years of my life, comrade, and stand up—take more—more—You'll have to forgive me, comrade. I'll do all I can. I'll write to your parents—I'll write to—I can't do it—I can't—if I don't know who you are, I may be able to forget you—time will wipe out the memory of you. But if I learn your name, it will always stand before me—accusing me. I'll write to your wife—I'll write to her—she must hear it from me! I promise you she shall not want for anything—I will tell her everything I have told you—I will help her—and your parents too—only forgive me! Forgive me!

World War II

WHY WE FIGHT

A sermon supports the troops on a Battleground.

Chaplain: Well, now it's almost Christmas, and here we are in beautiful Bastagne, enjoying the winter sports. And the $64 question is: "Was this trip necessary?" I'll try to answer that. But my sermons, like everything else in the army, depend on the situation and the terrain—so I can assure you this is going to be a quickie! Was this trip necessary? Well, let's look at the facts. A strong evil force got going in the world—something we call Fascism, Nazism. Nobody wanted this war except the Nazis. A great many people tried to deal with them, and a lot of them are dead—millions have died for no reason except that the Nazis wanted them dead. When we came to the final showdown, there wasn't anything to do but fight . . . There's a great lesson in this, and those of us who are learning it the hard way are not going to forget it. We must never again let any kind of force dedicated to a super race or a super idea or a super anything get strong enough to impose itself on a free world. We have to be smart enough and tough enough in the beginning to put out the fire before it starts spreading . . . My answer to the $64 question is, "Yes, this trip was necessary! And don't let anyone ever tell you it wasn't! . . . And now, Jerry permitting, let us pray—let us pray for the fog to lift. Almighty God . . . The organist is hitting those bass notes a little too loud for me to be heard, so let us each pray in his own way—to his own god.

WHY GO TO WAR

Andy Hardy's Blonde Trouble *is minor compared to the consequences of enlistment.*

Emily: Why, why should Andy go to war?

Judge Hardy: Emily, for the same reason I fought—and my father fought. Perhaps I can best explain it with the words from the first chapter of Genesis: "God created man in his own image." But those we're fighting want to create a world in their own image, a world of tyranny, cruelty, and slavery. We're not fighting this war for a conquest, Emily, but to make a world that will be safe for our children. We're fighting for tolerance and decency, and for the four freedoms that the president of the United States has so simply stated. It is to make this world safe that our nation has placed it in the hands and hearts of our millions of free men and women. Your son, Andrew, is one of those millions.

THE SCHOOLTEACHER

In the midst of World War II, a French film director (Jean Renoir), an English character actor (Charles Laughton), and an American film company (RKO) combined to make a propaganda film about the German occupation of a French town. That some critics find This Land Is Mine *to be "dated and disappointing" (see Leonard Maltin's* Film and Video Guide) *is a disgrace. The Nazis were defeated long ago, but men of character continue to wrestle with complex choices in dangerous circumstances. The decision to take a stand for freedom at the cost of one's own life is never "dated."*

Sorel: Like all young men I fell in love, but . . . she died . . . And I found a great comfort in my work. *Our* work. My family became this school—my books, my teachers—you, Miss Martin—my pupils—many of them grown up now. You know, it's a great thing to be a schoolmaster. It's a life-work. You sacrifice a lot of things, but you get a lot in return. And now I believe we're the most important people in our country. It's a time for sacrifice now, more than ever—and our real happiness lies in our doing our job well. Our mayor was in here this morning, talking about duty—but I prefer to use the word *job*. Those books must be burned. Very well, we must burn them—We can't resist physically. But morally, within us, we can resist. We contain those books, we contain truth, and they can't destroy truth without destroying each and every one of us. We can keep truth alive if the children believe in us and follow our example. Children like to follow a leader—and they have two kinds of leaders today. We seem weak, we have no weapons, we don't march—except to air raid shelters—and our heroes are called criminals and shot against walls. The other leaders have guns, tanks, parades, uniforms; they teach violence, self-love, vanity—everything that appeals to the unformed minds of children—and their criminals are called heroes. That's a lot of competition for us. Love of liberty isn't glamorous to children. Respect for the human being isn't exciting. But there's one weapon they can't take away from us—and that's our own dignity. It's going to be a fight—it is a fight, but if the children admire us they will follow us. We will win, Mr. Lory—or maybe we will get shot. But every one of us they execute wins a battle for our cause, because he dies a hero. And heroism is glamorous for the children. I don't ask you to die, my friend. Not immediately. But if you think these things over, I'm sure it will help you when we have trouble.

A SILLY OLD MAN

Arrested for a murder he did not commit, a young Charles Laughton makes his final statement to the court and the citizens of his small, occupied town.

Albert: I hope you'll excuse me if I speak badly; I've never been able to speak in public. I know the prosecutor has been making fun of me. I realize now that it's very easy to make fun of me—because I am ridiculous. I've always known I was ridiculous. And it's true I was jealous. That's ridiculous. I realize now I deserve to be laughed at—oh, not for loving a young girl, no one could help loving her, and it's a beautiful thing to love someone—but it was silly of me to have hopes, to dream that she would ever accept me. Being alone in my cell these days and nights, thinking, I've learned a lot of things. We forget what we look like. We imagine we're still young, even when we grow old. But this morning when I shaved, I looked at myself, and I saw a very silly old man. But even that doesn't help things—you go on loving. But that's not what I'm on trial for. I'm guilty of folly, but not of murder. I hope the prosecutor won't think I'm disrespectful to this court and the legal profession in not having a lawyer. My only defense is the truth. And no lawyer could know the truth as well as I do, because I was there. I was the only one who was there. I've always believed in the truth. Only sometimes you're blind and you can't see it. But then when somebody tells you, it's all clear, and you realize how stupid you were in believing lies. The truth is I wanted to kill George Lambert. But I don't think I could have. I'm too weak. I'm a coward. Everyone knows it, even the prosecutor—that's why he makes fun of me. (*touching his heart earnestly*) Oh, I'm not a coward in here. I have brave dreams, I'm not afraid to commit a murder here. (*touches his head*) But when I face reality outside, I'm lost, I'm a coward. It's so strange. We're two people, all of us. One inside and one outside. George Lambert was two men. It wasn't till I saw him dead that I realized it—and I knew why he'd killed himself. He couldn't face reality. He was different from me: He was strong outside and weak inside. Inside *he* was a coward. And when this honest coward had to face what the other George, the brave George, had done, he couldn't stand it. So he killed himself. It's strange, but I felt strong for the first time in my life when I saw him dead. And I was sorry for him. I suddenly understood everything. In a way, I was responsible for his death—through my mother's love for me. Even love can be a terrible thing—it can commit crimes. Louise, you thought I informed on Paul. It was my mother. To save me, she told George. George told the mayor who told Major von Keller, and Paul was killed. Even Mayor Manville is two men—they both appear to be strong, but they're both weak. The outside man has to pretend he's saving the town to hide the inside man who is saving himself . . . Even before the war, our major was convinced that our enemy was not the Germans but a part of our own people. Our mayor was born poor and then he became powerful—and he began to fear the very people he'd come from. Our country is full of men like that;—every country is. George Lambert wasn't powerful—but he chose the side of the powerful men. He honestly and sincerely admired them, and he found he got along better that way . . .

NAZI PROPAGANDA

Interrupted, the professor spends a final evening in jail. Worried that he'll be just as eloquent in court when he resumes his testimonies, the Nazis offer him a deal, with explanations.

von Keller: My dear Lory, it's a peculiar situation. A courtroom is a public forum. Of course, we Germans could take over courts, schools, town halls, the administration of the whole country. But we're not tyrants—we prefer not to do that. We prefer to collaborate, to give freedom to the nations we defeat on the battlefield. But freedom must be limited by the necessities of war. We're still fighting on other fronts. It's a very small sacrifice we ask of you, when we are still sacrificing our lives for the future happiness of the world. You see, I'm frank, I have nothing to conceal. I tell you these things because you're a man of intelligence. Lambert was just a tool, very honest, but not very bright. The mayor—you were right in the courtroom—he's working for his own interests. But—we need them and we find them in every country we invade. Even in Germany. That was the way our party got into power. They're everywhere. That's why we'll eventually control the world. America feels secure because of her oceans—they think of invasion in terms of armies and airplanes—but they're already invaded. The honest Lamberts and the dishonest Manvilles are waiting to welcome us—just as they did here. And if at any time we need peace—if peace should be a further weapon of conquest—their sincere patriotism will find plenty of arguments for the peace. After all, what is the United States? A charming cocktail of Irish and Jews. Very spectacular, but very childish. And England? A few old ladies wearing their grandfathers' leather britches.

THE CONFESSION

Albert doesn't buy it and, despite attempts to stop him, the judge allows him his final day in court.

Albert: I'm a very lucky man. I had a moment of weakness last night—I wanted to live. And I had good reasons to live. Major von Keller told me beautiful things about the future of this world they're building now. I almost believed him. It's very hard for people like you and me to understand what is evil and what is good. It's easy for working people to know who the enemy is because the aim of this war and this occupation is to make them slaves. But middle class people like us can easily believe as George Lambert did—that a German victory isn't such a bad thing. You hear people say that too much liberty brings chaos and disorder. That's why I was tempted last night by Major von Keller when he came to my cell. But this morning I looked out through bars and saw this beautiful new world working. I saw ten men die because they still believed in freedom—and among them was a man I loved, Professor Sorel. He smiled and waved to me, as if he were telling me what to do. I knew then I had to die—and the strange thing is, I was happy . . . Those ten men died because of Paul Martin—But they didn't blame Paul Martin—they were proud of him. Paul was a soldier. Without glory but in a wonderful cause. I see now that sabotage is the only weapon left to a defeated people—and so long as we have saboteurs the other free nations who are still fighting on the battlefields will know that we're not defeated. I know that for every German killed, many of our innocent citizens are executed. But the example of their heroism is contagious, and our resistance grows. It's very easy to talk about heroism in the free countries. But it's hard to talk about it here where our people are starving. The hard truth is that the hungrier we get the more we need our heroes. We must top saying that sabotage is wrong, that it doesn't pay—it does pay. It makes us suffer, starve, and die—but though it increases our misery, it will shorten our slavery. That's a hard choice, I know. But even now they are bringing more troops into this town because of the trouble that has started—and the more German soldiers here, the less they have on the fighting fronts. Even an occupied town like this can be a fighting front, too—and the fighting is harder. We not only have to fight hunger and a tyrant—first we have to fight ourselves. This occupation—any occupation in any land—is only possible because we are corrupt. I accuse myself first. The flesh is weak. For my own comfort and security I made no protest against the mutilation of truth in our school books. My mother got me extra food—and milk—by a subterfuge, and I accepted it without facing the fact that I was depriving children and people poorer than we were of their portion . . . You are the butcher, Mr. Noble. Naturally, you wanted to survive—and the black market was the answer. You keep your business going by selling meat out the back door at ten times its price. Some to my mother, who was equally guilty, as I was in eating it . . . You, Mr. Milette, are doing very well with your hotel, even though it's filled with Germans. You've never sold so much champagne, and at such a good price. Of course they print the money for nothing, but with this money you're buying properties, just as the mayor is. I could say the same about many of you. If the occupation lasts long enough, the men who are taking advantage of it will own the town. I don't blame you for making money—you should blame yourselves for making the occupation possible. Because you can't do these things without playing into the hands of the real rulers of the town, the Germans . . . That's why I know you must condemn me to die. Not because I killed George Lambert, which I didn't, but because I've tried to tell the truth. And the truth can't be allowed to live under the occupation. It's too dangerous. This occupation lives upon lies, just as the whole evil world they call the New Order does. Officially you will find me guilty of murder. But don't worry, my friends, even if you acquitted me and I walked out of this courtroom a free man, the enemy would take me and put me against a wall. And you, too. They can find any reasons to take hostages. There's one final charge I must answer to, and I'm very guilty. Yesterday, I was ashamed when the prosecutor accused me of loving you, Louise . . . It's true. I've always loved you, secretly. But now I'm not ashamed, I'm proud, and I don't want to keep it a secret. I want to tell the whole world . . . I don't feel silly at all. Maybe it's because I'm going to die—but I feel very young now. Last night Major von Keller told me something very funny: He told me I wasn't a coward—I think he was right . . . And I think I'm not the only one who's not a coward— this town is full of courage. I'm proud of it. I'm proud to be born and die here. Thank you, your honors.

FASCISM

Here is a more compact expression of those sentiments. Lillian Hellman's play Watch on the Rhine *was adapted for film by Hellman and her lover Dashiell Hammett, both of whom were "premature anti-fascists" and staunch advocates for the freedom of man everywhere.*

Kurt: Hitler alone is not what is wrong: let us not make too much of him. And not alone Nazism, either. But all fascist doing and thinking, by whatever name you wish to call it, and all that brings it about.

ON WAR

American Navy officer Charlie Madison finds himself in love in London during the blitz, with a British ambulance driver. Though at first she harbors anti-American attitudes, Charlie quickly disabuses her of her prejudice, beginning The Americanization of Emily.

Madison: You American-haters bore me to tears, Miss Barham. I've dealt with Europeans all my life. I know all about us parvenus from the States, who come over here and race around your old cathedral towns with our cameras and Coca-Cola bottles, brawl in your pubs, paw your women, and act like we own the world. We over-tip, we talk too loud, we think we can buy anything with a Hershey bar. I've had Germans and Italians tell me how politically ingenuous we are. Perhaps so, but we haven't managed a Hitler or a Mussolini yet. I've had Frenchmen call me a savage because I only took half an hour for lunch. Hell, Miss Barham, the only reason the French take two hours for lunch is because the service in their restaurants is lousy. And the most tedious of the lot are you British. We crass Americans didn't introduce war into your little island. This war, Miss Barham, to which we Americans are so insensitive, is the result of two thousand years of European greed, barbarism, superstition, and stupidity. Don't blame it on our Coca-Cola bottles. Europe was a going brothel long before we came to town.

Eventually he meets her mother, a woman living in the past who has lost her family to wars. We learn how Charlie, formerly a procurer for the needs of hotel guests, obtained his cushy position as Admiral's Dogbody.

Madison: I was offered all sorts of commissions in the Army and Navy, the one I have now, in fact. Admiral Jessup phoned me to join his staff. But I had always been a little embarrassed by my job at the hotel and wanted to do something redeeming. Have you noticed that war is the only chance a man gets to do something redeeming? That's why war's so attractive.

Mrs. Braham: Yes, war is very handsome, I quite agree.

Madison: At any rate, I turned down Admiral Jessup's offer and enlisted in the marines as a pirate. I even applied for combat service. My wife, to all appearances a perfectly sensible woman, encouraged me in this idiotic decision. Seven months later, I found myself invading the Solomon Islands. There I was, splashing away in the shoals of Guadalcanal. It suddenly occurred to me a man could get killed doing this kind of thing. The fact is, most of the men splashing along with me were screaming in agony and dying like flies. I don't think any of them wanted to die. Yet they had all volunteered for the Marines, and the odds on getting killed are pretty good in the Marines. To make it more grotesque, their wives, sweethearts, and mothers had all applauded their acts of suicide, and their children were proud of them for it. It was then I realized how admirable war was, the most admirable act of man. Those were brave men dying there. In peacetime, they had all been normal, decent cowards, frightened of their wives, trembling before their bosses, terrified at the passing of the years. But war had made them gallant. They had been greedy men; now they were self-sacrificing. They had been selfish; now they were generous. Hell, war isn't hell at all. It's man at his best, the highest morality he is capable of.

But Charlie is wise to the absurdity of it all.

Madison: It's not war that's insane, you see; it's the morality of it. It's not greed and ambition that makes wars—it's goodness. Wars are always fought for the best of reasons, for liberation or manifest destiny, always against tyranny, and always in the interests of humanity. So far this war, we've managed to butcher some ten million humans in the interest of humanity. The next war, it seems, we'll have to destroy all of man in order to preserve his damn dignity. It's not war that is unnatural to us—it's virtue. As long as valor remains a virtue, we shall have soldiers. So, I preach cowardice. Through cowardice we shall all be saved.

And he has a solution.

Madison: We shall never end wars, Mrs. Barham, by blaming it on ministers and generals or warmongering imperialists or all the other banal bogies. It's the rest of us who build statues to those generals and name boulevards after those ministers. It's the rest of us who make heroes of our dead and shrines of our battlefields. We wear our widow's weeds like nuns, Mrs. Barham, and perpetuate war by exalting its sacrifices. It may be ministers and generals who blunder us into wars, Mrs. Barham, but the least the rest of us can do is to resist honoring the institution. What has my mother got for pretending bravery was admirable? She is under constant sedation and terrified she might wake up one morning and find her last son has run off to be brave.

WAR CRIMINALS

Judgment at Nuremberg is a dramatization of the Nazi war crime trials that followed World War II. The prosecutor is the first to state his case.

Colonel Lawson: The case is unusual in that the defendants are charged with crimes committed in the name of the law. These men, together with their deceased or fugitive colleagues, are the embodiment of what passed for justice during the Third Reich. Therefore, you, Your Honors, as judges on the bench, will be sitting in judgment of judges in the dock. This is as it should be. For only a judge knows how much more a court is than a courtroom. It is a process and a spirit. It is the House of Law. The defendants knew this, too. They know courtrooms well. They sat in their black robes. And they distorted and they perverted and they destroyed justice and law in Germany. This, in itself, is undoubtedly a great crime. But the prosecution is not calling the defendants to account for violating constitutional guarantees or withholding due process of law. It is calling them to account for murder, brutalities, torture, atrocities. They share with all the leaders of the Third Reich responsibility for the most malignant, the most calculated, the most, devastating crimes in the history of mankind. They are perhaps more guilty than some others. They had attained maturity long before Hitler's rise to power. Their minds were not warped at an early age by Nazi teachings. They embraced the ideologies of the Third Reich as educated adults. They, most of all, should have valued justice. Here they will receive the justice they denied others. They will be judged according to the evidence presented in this courtroom. The prosecution asks nothing more.

Next, the defense has its chance.

Rolfe: May it please the tribunal. It is not only a great honor but also a great challenge for an advocate to aid this tribunal in its task. For this is not an ordinary trial, by any means, of the accepted parochial sense. The avowed purpose of this Tribunal is broader than the visiting of retribution on a few men. It is dedicated to the reconsecration of the Temple of Justice. It is dedicated to finding a code of justice the whole world will be responsible to. How will this code be established? It will be established in a clear, honest evaluation of the responsibility for the crimes in the indictment stated by the prosecution. In the words of the great American jurist, Oliver Wendell Holmes, "This responsibility will not be found only in documents that no one contests or denies. It will be found in consideration of a political or social nature. It will be found, most of all, in the character of men." What is the character of Ernst Janning? Let us examine his life for a moment. He was born in 1895. Received the degree of Doctor of Law in 1917. Became a judge in East Prussia in 1924. Following World War One, he became one of the leaders of the Weimar Republic and was one of the framers of its democratic constitution. In subsequent years he achieved international fame. Not only for his work as a great jurist, but also as the author of legal textbooks which are still used in universities all over the world. He became Minister of Justice in Germany in 1935. A position the equivalent of the Attorney General of the United States. Finally, in a Reichstag speech of 26 April 1942, Hitler attacked Janning and forced him to resign. If Ernst Janning is to be found guilty, certain implications must arise. A judge does not make the law. He carries out the laws of his country. The statement, "My country right or wrong," was expressed by a great American patriot. It is no less true for a German patriot. Should Ernst Janning have carried out the laws of his country? Or should he have refused to carry them out and become a traitor? This is the crux of the issue at the bottom of this trial. The defense is as dedicated to finding responsibility as is the prosecution. For it is not only Ernst Janning who is on trial here. It is the German people.

The prosecutor makes an apology.

Colonel Lawson: There's one thing about Americans. We're not cut out to be occupiers. We're new at it and we're not very good at it. We come here. We see this beautiful country—and it is beautiful—we see the culture that goes back hundreds of years. We see its *gemütlich* charm, and the charm of people like Mrs. Bertholt. We have a built-in inferiority complex. We forgive and forget easy. We give the other guy the benefit of the doubt. That's the American way. We beat the greatest war machine since Alexander the Great—and now the Boy Scouts take over.

But the man in the dock doesn't believe in his own innocence.

Janning: I wish to testify about the Feldenstein case because it was the most significant trial of the period. It is important not only for the tribunal to understand it, but the German people. But to understand it, one must understand the period in which it happened. There was a fever over the land. A fever of disgrace, of indignity, of hunger. We had a democracy, yes, but it was torn by elements within. There was, above all, fear. Fear of today, fear of tomorrow, fear of our neighbors, fear of ourselves. Only when you understand that can you understand what Hitler meant to us. Because he said to us: Lift your heads! Be proud to be German! There are devils among us! Communists, liberals, Jews, Gypsies—once the devils will be destroyed, your miseries will be destroyed. It was the old, old story of the sacrificial lamb. What about those of us who knew better? We, who knew the words were lies and worse than lies? Why did we sit silent? Why did we participate? Because we loved our country. What difference does it make if a few political extremists lose their rights? What difference does it make if a few racial minorities lose their rights? It is only a passing phase. It is only a stage we are going through. It will be discarded sooner or later. Hitler himself will be discarded sooner or later. "The country is in danger." We will "march out of the shadows." We will "go forward." And history tells how well we succeeded, your Honor! We succeeded beyond our wildest dreams. The very elements of hate and power about Hitler that mesmerized Germany mesmerized the world! We found ourselves with sudden powerful allies. Things that had been denied us as a democracy were open to us now. The world said, go ahead, take it! Take Sudetenland, take the Rhineland—remilitarize it—take all of Austria, take it! We marched forward. The danger passed. And then, one day, we looked around and found we were in an even more terrible danger. The rites began in this courtroom, swept over our land like a raging, roaring disease! What was going to be a passing phase had become a way of life. Your Honor, I was content to sit silent during this trial. I was content to tend my roses. I was even content to let counsel try to save my name. Until I realized that in order to save it, he would have to raise the specter again. You have seen him do it. He has done it in this courtroom. He has suggested that the Third Reich worked for the benefit of people. He has suggested that we sterilized men for the welfare of the country. He has suggested that perhaps the old Jew did sleep with the sixteen-year-old girl after all. Once more it is being done out of love of the country. It is not easy to tell the truth. But if there is to be any salvation for Germany, those of us who know our guilt must admit it, no matter the cost in pain and humiliation. I had reached my verdict on the Feldenstein case before I ever came into the courtroom. I would have found him guilty, whatever the evidence. It was not a trial at all. It was a sacrificial ritual in which Feldenstein, the Jew, was the helpless victim. My defense counsel would have you believe that we were not aware of concentration camps? Not aware? Where were we? Where were we when Hitler began shrieking his hate in the Reichstag? Where were we when our neighbors were being dragged out in the middle of the night to Dachau? Where were we when every village in Germany had a railroad terminal where cattle-cars were filled with children who were being carried off to their extermination? Where were we when they cried out into the night to us? Were we deaf, dumb, and blind?—My counsel says we were not aware of the extermination of millions. He would give you the excuse we were only aware of the extermination of hundreds. Does that make us any the less guilty? Maybe we didn't know the details. But if we didn't know, it was because we didn't want to know.

This makes for a tough client to defend. Counsel makes a final, desperate argument.

Rolfe: Your honors, my duty is to defend Ernst Janning. And yet, Ernst Janning has said he is guilty. There is no doubt he feels his guilt. He made a terrible mistake in going along with the Nazi movement, hoping it would be good for his country. But . . . If he is to be found guilty, there are others who also went along who must also be found guilty. Herr Janning said we succeeded beyond our wildest dreams. Why did we succeed? What about the rest of the world, your Honors? Did they not know the intentions of the Third Reich? Did they not hear the words of Hitler broadcast all over the world? Did they not read his intentions in *Mein Kampf*, published in every corner of the world? Where is the responsibility of the Soviet Union, who in 1939 signed a pact with Hitler and enabled him to make war? Are we now to find Russia guilty? Where is the responsibility of the Vatican,

who signed the Concordat Pact in 1933 with Hitler, giving him his first tremendous prestige? Are we now to find the Vatican guilty? Where is the responsibility of the world leader, Winston Churchill, who said in an open letter to the London *Times* in 1938— 1938, your Honors! "Were England to suffer a national disaster, I should pray to God to send a man of the strength of mind and will of an Adolf Hitler." Are we now to find Winston Churchill guilty? Where is the responsibility of those American industrialists who helped Hitler to rebuild his arms and profited by that rebuilding? Are we to find the American industrialists guilty? No, your Honor. Germany alone is not guilty. The whole world is as responsible for Hitler as Germany. It is an easy thing to condemn one man in the dock. It is easy to condemn the German people—to speak of the "basic flaw" in the German character that allowed Hitler to rise to power—and at the same time comfortably ignore the "basic flaw" of character that made the

Russians sign pacts with him, Winston Churchill praise him, American industrialists profit by him! Ernst Janning says he is guilty. If he is, Ernst Janning's guilt is the world's guilt. No more and no less.

THE KINGDOM OF GOD IS IN MAN

In his first talkie, Charlie Chaplin wrote for himself not one but two great parts: Adenoid Hynkel, The Great Dictator *of Tomania, and a much wiser, if less warlike, local Jewish barber, who happens to resemble Herr Hynkel. Mistaken identify puts the barber on the podium, and the world receives a moral lesson.*

The Barber: I'm sorry, but I don't want to be an emperor; that's not my business. I don't want to rule or conquer anyone. I should like to help everyone, if possible. Jew, gentile, black, white. We all want to help one another; human beings are like that. We want to live by each other's happiness, not by each other's misery. We don't want to hate and despise one another. In this world there's room for everyone, and the good world is rich and can provide for everyone. The way of life can be free and beautiful. But we have lost the way. Greed has poisoned men's souls, has barricaded the world with hate, has goose-stepped us into misery and bloodshed. We have developed speed but we have shut ourselves in. Machinery that gives abundance has left us in want. Our knowledge has made us cynical; our cleverness, hard and unkind. We think too much and feel too little. More than machinery, we need humanity. More than cleverness, we need kindness and gentleness. Without these qualities, life will be violent and all will be lost. The airplane and the radio have brought us closer together; the very nature of these inventions cries out for the goodness in men. Cries out for universal brotherhood for the unity of us all. Even now, my voice is reaching millions throughout the world—millions of despairing men, women, and little children, victims of a system that makes men torture and imprison innocent people. To those who can hear me, I say, "Do not despair." The misery that is now upon us is but the passing of greed, the bitterness of men who fear the way of human progress. The hate of men will pass, and dictators die. And the power they took from the people will return to the people. And so long as men die, liberty will never perish.

Soldiers, don't give yourself to brutes. Men who despise you, enslave you, who regiment your lives, tell you what to do, what to think, and what to feel. Who drill you, diet you, treat you like cattle, use you as cannon fodder. Don't give yourselves to these unnatural men. Machine men with machine minds and machine hearts! You are not machines, you are not cattle, you are men! You have the love of humanity in your hearts—you don't hate. Only the unloved hate. The unloved and the unnatural! Soldiers, don't fight for slavery! Fight for liberty! In the seventeenth chapter of St. Luke, it is written: The Kingdom of God is in man. Not one man, nor a group of men, but in all men. In you—you, the people, have the power. The power to create machines, the power to create happiness. You, the people, have the power to make this life free and beautiful, to make this life a wonderful adventure! Then, in the name of democracy, let us use that power! Let us all unite! Let us fight for a new world. A decent world that will give man a chance to work, that will give you the future and old age of security. By the promise of these things, brutes have risen to power. But they lie. They do not fulfill that promise. They never will. Dictators free themselves, but they enslave the people. Now let us fight to fulfill that promise! Let us fight to free the world! To do away with greed, with hate and intolerance.

Let us fight for a world of reason, a world where science and progress lead to all men's happiness. Soldiers! In the name of democracy, let us all unite! Hannah? Can you hear me? Wherever you are? Look up, Hannah. The clouds are lifting. The sun is breaking through. We are coming out of the darkness into the light. We are coming into a new world, a kind new world. Where men will rise above their hate, their greed and brutality. Look up, Hannah, the soul of man has been given wings! And at last he is beginning to fly. He is flying into the rainbow, into the light of hope, into the future—the glorious future that belongs to you, to me, and to all others. Look up Hannah . . . Look up . . .

The Cold War

THE WORLD HAS WALLS

Among A Few Good Men, *Colonel Nathan R. Jessep is one of the old-timers. In charge of the American naval base on the edge of Cuba, he is nose-to-nose with the enemy and doesn't have much time for the investigation of an accidental death by Navy lawyers with cushy jobs.*

Jessep: Son, we live in a world that has walls. And those walls have to be guarded by men with guns. Who's gonna do it? You? You, Lt. Weinberg? I have a greater responsibility than you can possibly fathom. You weep for Santiago and you curse the Marines. You have that luxury. You have the luxury of not knowing what I know: that Santiago's death, while tragic, probably saved lives. And my existence, while grotesque and incomprehensible to you, saves lives. You don't want the truth. Because deep down, in places you don't talk about at parties, you want me on that wall. You want me there. We use words like honor, code, loyalty. We use these words as the backbone to a life spent defending something. You use 'em as a punchline. I have neither the time nor the inclination to explain myself to a man who rises and sleeps under the blanket of the very freedom I provide, then questions the manner in which I provide it. I'd prefer you just said thank you and went on your way. Otherwise, I suggest you pick up a weapon and stand a post. Either way, I don't give a damn what you think you're entitled to.

YOUR COMMIE

At the height of the Cold War, Dr. Strangelove *posed the possibility of a failure of Fail Safe, the Pentagon policy whereby nuclear war wasn't supposed to happen by accident. In this case, General Jack D. Ripper goes ahead and orders an attack on his own authority because . . .*

Ripper: Your commie has no regard for human life, not even his own. And for this reason, men, I want to impress upon you the need for extreme watchfulness. The enemy may come individually or he may come in strength. He may even come in the uniform of our own troops. But, however he comes, we must stop him. We must not allow him to gain entrance to this base. Now, I am going to give you three simple rules: First, trust no one, whatever his uniform or rank, unless he is known to you personally. Second, anyone or anything that approaches within 200 yards of the perimeter is to be fired upon. Third, if in doubt, shoot first and ask questions afterwards. I would sooner accept a few casualties through accident than lose the entire base and its personnel through carelessness. Any variation on these rules must come from me personally. Now, men, in conclusion, I would like to say that, in the two years it has been my privilege to be your commanding officer, I have always expected the best from you, and you have never given me anything less than that.

ACCEPTABLE CIVILIAN CASUALTIES

When the administration discovers what Ripper has done, they huddle in the War Room ("Gentlemen, you can't fight in here, this is the war room!") to frame an official response. The Air Force, in the person of General "Buck" Turgidson, strongly advises that America jump in with both feet.

Turgidson: One: Our hopes for recalling the 843rd bomb wing are quickly being reduced to a very low order of probability. Two, in less than fifteen minutes from now the Russkies will be making radar contact with the planes. Three, when they do, they are going to go absolutely ape, and they're gonna strike back with everything they've got. Four, if, prior to this time, we have done nothing further to suppress their retaliatory capabilities, we will suffer virtual annihilation. Now, five, if, on the other hand we were to immediately launch an all-out and coordinated attack on all their airfields and missile bases, we'd stand a damn good chance of catching 'em with their pants down. Hell, we got a five-to-one missile superiority as it is. We could easily assign three missiles to every target and still have a very effective reserve force for any other contingency. Now, six: An unofficial study which we undertook of this eventuality indicated that we would destroy ninety percent of their nuclear capabilities. We would therefore prevail, and suffer only modest and acceptable civilian casualties from their remaining force, which would be badly damaged and uncoordinated.

HELLO, DIMITRI?

But the President prefers moderation. He telephones his counterpart in the Soviet Union.

Muffley: Hello? Hello, Dimitri? Listen, I can't hear too well, do you suppose you could turn the music down just a little? Oh, that's much better. Yes. Fine, I can hear you now, Dimitri. Clear and plain and coming through fine. I'm coming through fine, too, eh? Good, then. Well, then, as you say, we're both coming through fine. Good. Well, it's good that you're fine and I'm fine. I agree with you. It's great to be fine. Now then, Dimitri. You know how we've always talked about the possibility of something going wrong with the bomb. The bomb, Dimitri. The hydrogen bomb. Well, now, what happened is, one of our base commanders, he had a sort of, well, he went a little funny in the head. You know. Just a little . . . funny. And, uh, he went and did a silly thing. Well, I'll tell you what he did, he ordered his planes . . . to attack your country. Well let me finish, Dimitri. Let me finish, Dimitri. Well, listen, how do you think I feel about it? Can you imagine how I feel about it, Dimitri? Why do you think I'm calling you? Just to say hello? Of course I like to speak to you. Of course I like to say hello. Not now, but any time, Dimitri. I'm just calling up to tell you something terrible has happened. It's a friendly call. Of course it's a friendly call. Listen, if it wasn't friendly, you probably wouldn't have even got it. They will not reach their targets for at least another hour. I am . . . I am positive, Dimitri. Listen, I've been all over this with your ambassador. It is not a trick. Well, I'll tell you. We'd like to give your air staff a complete rundown on the targets, the flight plans, and the defensive systems of the planes. Yes! I mean, if we're unable to recall the planes then I'd say that, uh, well, we're just going to have to help you destroy them, Dimitri. I know they're our boys. All Right, well, listen . . . who should we call? Who should we call, Dimitri? The people...? Sorry, you faded away there. The People's Central Air Defense Headquarters. Where is that, Dimitri? In Omsk. Right. Yes. Oh, you'll call them first, will you? Uh huh. Listen, do you happen to have the phone number on you, Dimitri? What? I see, just ask for Omsk Information. I'm sorry, too, Dimitri. I'm very sorry. All Right! You're sorrier than I am! But I am sorry, as well. I am as sorry as you are, Dimitri. Don't say that you are more sorry than I am, because I am capable of being just as sorry as you are. So we're both sorry, all right? All right. Yes, he's right here. Yes, he wants to talk to you. Just a second . . .

Vietnam

WAR IS HELL

In Vietnam, several soldiers in the same Platoon *have different views of that war.*

Chris: Somebody once wrote, "Hell is the impossibility of reason." That's what this place feels like. I hate it already and it's only been a week. Some goddamn week, Grandma . . . The hardest thing I think I've ever done is go on point three times this week—I don't even know what I'm doing. A gook could be standing three feet in front of me and I wouldn't know it, I'm so tired. We get up at five a.m., hump all day, camp around four or five p.m., dig foxhole, eat, then put out an all-night ambush or a three-man listening post in the jungle. It's scary, 'cause nobody tells me how to do anything 'cause I'm new and nobody cares about the new guys; they don't even want to know your name. The unwritten rule is a new guy's life isn't worth as much 'cause he hasn't put his time in yet—and they say, if you're gonna get killed in Nam, it's better to get it in the first few weeks, the logic being you don't suffer that much. I can believe that . . . If you're lucky, you get to stay in the perimeter at night and then you pull a three-hour guard shift, so maybe you sleep three–four hours a night, but you don't really sleep . . . I don't think I can keep this up for a year, Grandma—I think I've made a big mistake coming here . . . 'Course, Mom and Dad didn't want me to come, they wanted me to be just like them—respectable, hard-working, making $200 a week, a little house, a family. They drove me crazy with their goddamn world, Grandma, you know Mom; I don't want to be a white boy on Wall Street, I don't want my whole life to be predetermined by them . . . I guess I have always been sheltered and special. I just want to be anonymous. Like everybody else. Do my share for my country. Live up to what Grandpa did in the First World War and Dad the Second. I know this is going to be the war of my generation. Well, here I am—anonymous all right, with guys nobody really cares about.—They come from the end of the line, most of 'em, small towns you never heard of—Pulaski, Tennessee; Brandon, Mississippi; Pork Bend, Utah; Wampum, Pennsylvania. Two years' high school's about it, maybe if they're lucky a job waiting for 'em back in a factory but most of 'em got nothing. They're poor, they're the unwanted of our society, yet they're fighting for our society and our freedom, and what we call America. They're the bottom of the barrel—and they know it, maybe that's why they call themselves "grunts" cause a "grunt" can take it, can take anything. They're the backbone of this country, Grandma, the best I've ever seen, the heart and soul.—I've found I finally, way down here in the mud— maybe from down here I can start up again and be something I can be proud of, without having to fake it, maybe . . . I can see something I don't yet see, learn something I don't yet know . . . I miss you, I miss you very much, tell Mom I miss her too. Chris.

A black soldier has his own perspective.

Rhah: Baaa! Fuck it they sold us out—so what! What'd you all expect? Civilian life is phony BULLSHIT, man. They're ROBOTS, man—watchin' dopey television and drivin' dopey cars, and they fuck up, nobody dies. That's all right, you keep fuckin' up, politicians keep lyin'. 'Cause it don't really matter. Don't mean shit. So what! Whatcha want—a parade! Fuck that, too! No grunt never got no respect. Till he was dead—and even THEN! You're fighting for YOURSELF, man! You're fighting for your SOUL, that's all. Remember that. And it's some goddamned battle too.—If you's a man, wrestle with that angle . . . love and hate—the whole shitbag show, that's the story then and now, and it ain't hardly gonna change . . .

This soldier is smoking a joint, which may explain why he's a bit more clear-headed about Vietnam.

Elias: We been kicking other people's asses so long, I guess it's time we got our own kicked. The only decent thing I can see coming out of here are the survivors—hundreds of thousands of guys like you, Taylor, going back to every little town in the country, knowing something about what it's like to take a life and what that can do to a person's soul—twist it like Barnes and Bunny and make 'em sick inside. And if you got any brains, you gonna fight it the rest of your life 'cause it's cheap, killing is cheap, the cheapest thing I know. And when some drunk like O'Neill starts glorifying it, you're gonna puke all over him. And when the politicians start selling you a used war all over again, you and your generation gonna say go fuck yourself , 'cause you know, you've seen it—and when you know it, deep down there, you know it till you die. That's why the survivors remember. 'Cause the dead don't let 'em forget.

THE ONLY HEROES

Perhaps Coming Home *is as difficult as it is to die over there.*

Luke: Listen, the only heroes of that war are the ones that didn't come back. The toughest thing that I have to live with is the fact that I killed a lot of people, and I got really into killing, and I dug it, and I see their faces at night sometimes. And there was a time I would have gone back just to get off doing that again. Thank God that's over. Thank God I feel bad about it. You know what I'm saying. Thank God I lived long enough to feel bad about it.

I'VE SEEN THE HORROR

Hollywood is supposedly populated with "bleeding-heart liberals." Screenwriter John Milius isn't one of them. In Apocalypse Now, *he and director Francis Ford Coppola define a renegade American soldier's admiration for the committed enemy.*

Kurtz: I've seen the horror. Horrors that you've seen. But you have no right to call me a murderer. You have no right to call me a murderer. You have a right to kill me. You have a right to do that, but you have no right to judge me. It's impossible for words to describe what is necessary to those who do not know what horror means. Horror. Horror has a face, and you must make a friend of horror. Horror and mortal terror are your friends. If they are not, then they are enemies to be feared. They are truly enemies. I remember when I was with Special Forces—it seems a thousand centuries ago—we went into a camp to inoculate it. The children. We left the camp after we had inoculated the children for polio and this old man came running after us, and he was crying. He couldn't see. We went there, and they had come and hacked off every inoculated arm. There they were, in a pile—a pile of little arms. And I remember . . . I . . . I . . . I cried, I wept like some grandmother. I wanted to tear my teeth out; I didn't know what I wanted to do. And I want to remember it, I never want to forget. And then I realized—like I was shot . . . like I was shot with a diamond . . . a diamond bullet right through my forehead. And I thought, "My God, the genius of that, the genius, the will to do that." Perfect, genuine, complete, crystalline, pure. And then I realized they could stand that—these were not monsters, these were men, trained contras, these men who fought with their hearts, who have families, who have children, who are filled with love—that they had this strength, the strength to do that. If I had ten divisions of those men, then our troubles here would be over very quickly. You have to have men who are moral and, at the same time, were able to utilize their primordial instincts to kill without feeling, without passion, without judgment—without judgment. Because it's judgment that defeats us. I worry that my son might not understand what I've tried to be, and if I were to be killed, Willard, I would want someone to go to my home and tell my son everything. Everything I did, everything you saw, because there's nothing that I detest more than the stench of lies. And if you understand me, Willard, you . . . you will do this for me.

Future Wars

GUN SALESMANSHIP

A search for The Fifth Element *requires weapons. Aknot gets a sales pitch from Zorg.*

Zorg: So what if the Federal Army crushed your entire race and scattered your people to the wind? Your time for revenge is at hand. Voila . . . the ZF1. It's light, the handle's adjustable for easy carrying, good for righties and lefties. Breaks down into four parts, undetectable by X-rays. It's the ideal weapon for quick, discreet interventions. A word on firepower: Titanium recharger. 3000-round clip with bursts of 3 to 300. With the replay button, another Zorg innovation, it's even easier. One shot, and replay sends every following shot to the same location. I recharge but the enemy has launched a cowardly sneak attack from behind; the auto mirror takes care of that. Gives me the time to turn around and finish the job. 300 round bursts, then there are the Zorg oldies. Rocket launcher. The always efficient flamethrower. My favorite. Our famous net launcher, the arrow launcher, with exploding or poisonous gas heads—very practical. And for the grand finale, the all-new ice-cube system! Four full crates, delivered right on time! What about you, my dear Aknot, did you bring me what I asked you for?

CHAPTER 6:

Rants

TO MY LISTENERS

Talk Radio is ubiquitous these days. This host takes a break from call-ins to let his audience know what they really mean to him.

Barry: Hold the calls. I'm here, I'm here every night, I come up here every night. This is my job, this is what I do for a living. I come up here and I do the best I can. I give you the best I can. I can't do better than this. I can't. I'm only a human being up here. I'm not God . . . uh . . . a lot of you out there are not . . . I may not be the most popular guy in the world. That's not the point. I really don't care what you think of me. I mean, who the hell are you anyways? You . . . "audience" . . . You call me up and you try to tell me things about myself. You don't know me. You don't know anything about me. You've never seen me. You don't know who I am, what I want, what I like, what I don't like in this world. I'm just a voice. A voice in the wilderness . . . And you . . . like a pack of baying wolves descend on me, 'cause you can't stand facing what it is you are and what you've made. Yes, the world is a terrible place! Yes, cancer and garbage disposals will get you! Yes, a war is coming. Yes, the world is shot to hell and you're all goners. Everything's screwed up, and you like it that way, don't you? You're fascinated by the gory details. You're mesmerized by your own fear! You revel in floods and car accidents and unstoppable diseases. You're happiest when others are in pain! And that's where I come in, isn't it? I'm here to lead you by the hand through the dark forest of your own hatred and anger and humiliation. I'm providing a public service! You're so scared! You're like the little child under the covers. You're afraid of the bogeyman but you can't live without him. Your fear, your own lives have become your entertainment! Tomorrow night millions of people are going to be listening to this show, and you have nothing to talk about! Marvelous technology is at our disposal and, instead of reaching up for new heights, we try to see how far down we can go, how deep into the muck we can immerse ourselves! What do you wanna talk about? Baseball scores? Your pet? Orgasms? You're pathetic. I despise each and every one of you. You've got nothing. Nothing. Absolutely nothing. No brains. No power. No future. No hope. No God. The only thing you believe in is me. What are you if you don't have me? I'm not afraid, see. I come up here every night and make my case, I make my point. I say what

I believe in. I have to, I have no choice, you frighten me! I come up here every night and I tear into you, I abuse you, I insult you . . . and you just keep calling. Why do you keep coming back, what's wrong with you? I don't want to hear any more, I've had enough. Stop talking. Don't call anymore! Go away! Bunch of yellow-bellied, spineless, bigoted, quivering, drunken, insomniatic, paranoid, disgusting, perverted, voyeuristic little obscene phone callers. That's what you are. Well, to hell with ya. I don't need your fear and your stupidity. You don't get it. It's wasted on you. Pearls before swine . . . (*catches his breath*) If one person out there had any idea what I'm talking about . . . (*Suddenly starts taking callers again*) Fred, you're on!

CONSUMERS

In Twelve Monkeys, *this mental patient has society figured out. Kids and lunatics say the darndest things.*

Jeffrey: A telephone call? That's communication with the outside world! Doctor's discretion. Hey, if alla these nuts could just make phone calls, it could spread. Insanity oozing through telephone cables, oozing into the ears of all those poor sane people, infecting them! Wackos everywhere! A plague of madness. In fact, very few of us here are actually mentally ill. I'm not saying you're not mentally ill, for all I know you're crazy as a loon. But that's not why you're here. Why you're here is because of the system, because of the economy. There's the TV. It's all right there. Commercials. We are not productive anymore, they don't need us to make things anymore, it's all automated. What are we for, then? We're consumers. Okay, buy a lot of stuff, you're a good citizen. But if you don't buy a lot of stuff, you know what? You're mentally ill! That's a fact! If you don't buy things . . . toilet paper, new cars, computerized blenders, electrically operated sexual devices . . . SCREWDRIVERS WITH MINIATURE BUILT-IN RADAR DEVICES, STEREO SYSTEMS WITH BRAIN-IMPLANTED HEADPHONES, VOICE-ACTIVATED COMPUTERS, AND . . . So if you want to watch a particular program, say "All My Children" or something, you go to the Charge Nurse and tell her what day and time the show you want to see is on. But you have to tell her before the show is scheduled to be on.

There was this one guy who was always requesting shows that had already played. He couldn't quite grasp the idea that the Charge Nurse couldn't just make it be yesterday for him, turn back time, ha ha. What a fruitcake!! Seriously, more and more people are being defined now as mentally ill. Why? Because they're not consuming on their own. But as patients they become consumers of mental health care. And this gives the so-called sane people work! WHOOO! SHOCK THERAPY! GROUP THERAPY! HALLUCINATIONS! THERAPEUTIC DRUGS! IGGIDY DIGGIDY DIG! PERFECT! THE SYSTEM IN HARMONY LIKE A BIG MACHINE...

A PSYCHIATRIST

But sometimes you wonder who's cracked, the patient or the psychiatrist.

Dr. Kathryn Railly: According to the accounts of local officials at that time, this gentleman, judged to be about forty years of age, appeared suddenly in the village of Wyle, near Stonehenge, in the west of England, in April of 1162. Using unfamiliar words and speaking in a strange accent, the man made dire prognostications about a pestilence, which he predicted would wipe out humanity in approximately 800 years. Deranged and hysterical, the man raped a young woman of the village, was taken into custody, but then mysteriously escaped and was not heard of again. In 1841 Mackay wrote, "During seasons of great pestilence, men have often believed the prophecies of crazed fanatics, that the end of the world was come." Obviously this plague/doomsday scenario is considerably more compelling when reality supports it in some form, whether it's the Bubonic Plague, smallpox, or AIDS. In addition to these "natural" contagions, there are now technological horrors as well. Besides radiation, consider our lurking fear of germ warfare and its close approximation, chemical warfare, which first reared its ugly head in the deadly mustard gas attacks during the First World War . . . During such an attack in the French trenches, in October 1917, we have an account of this soldier who, during an assault, was wounded by shrapnel and hospitalized behind the lines, where doctors discovered he had lost all comprehension of French but spoke English fluently, albeit in a regional dialect they didn't recognize.

The man, although physically unaffected by the gas, was hysterical. He claimed he had come from the future, that he was looking for a pure germ that would ultimately wipe mankind off the face of the earth in the year 1995! Although seriously injured, the young soldier disappeared from the hospital before more data could be gathered. No doubt he was trying to carry on his mission to warn others, substituting for the agony of war a self-inflicted agony we call the "Cassandra Complex." Cassandra, in Greek legend you will recall, was condemned to know the future but to be disbelieved when she foretold it. Hence, the agony of foreknowledge combined with impotence to do anything about it.

A TEACHER'S CREED

This schoolteacher in an impoverished neighborhood is always going Up the Down Staircase. *But he dispenses very good advice.*

Paul: They say a writer should stick to what he knows. What nonsense! What did Dickens know about the French Revolution? What did Shakespeare know about Moors in Venice? If he'd stuck to what he knew, we'd have no *Othello*. We'd have no *Treasure Island*, no *Alice in Wonderland*. You brats think I and Miss Barrett stand up here, day after day, talking about books and the writing of books just for the hell of it? You think it has nothing to do with you? A writer creates a book, an individual creates a life! For a writer to create a masterpiece, he has to think beyond what he knows! For you to create a life . . . even just a decent one . . . you have to go beyond what you know! Go beyond the poverty, diseases, dope, degeneracy, to the oceans, to the Alps *(points to a map)*, a magnificent replica of which the Board of Education has generously donated. Think, you damn numbskulls, or what the hell are you doing here? Stick to what you know, and *that's what you'll be stuck with!* You might as well get out! Now.

PROGRAMMING TELEVISION

A playwright who got his start in the golden days of live television drama, Paddy Chayefsky created characters that were articulate and very often angry. Network is his searing indictment of what television—particularly news-as-entertainment—has become. We start out with a television executive's analysis of what the public wants.

Diana: Why not? They've got Strike Force, Task Force, SWAT—why not Che Guevara and his own little mod squad? Listen, I sent you all a concept analysis report yesterday. Did any of you read it? (apparently not) Well, in a nutshell, it said the American people are turning sullen. They've been clobbered on all sides by Vietnam, Watergate, the inflation, the depression. They've turned off, shot up, and they've fucked themselves limp. And nothing helps. Evil still triumphs over all, Christ is a dope-dealing pimp, even sin turned out to be impotent. The whole world seems to be going nuts and flipping off into space like an abandoned balloon. So—this concept analysis report concludes—the American people want somebody to articulate their rage for them. I've been telling you people since I took this job six months ago that I want angry shows. I don't want conventional programming on this network. I want counterculture. I want anti-establishment.

THE MAD PROPHET INTRODUCES HIMSELF

News anchor Howard Beale has a meltdown when he's fired, then drives his ratings through the roof with his rantings as the "Mad Prophet of the Airwaves."

Howard: Last night, I was awakened from a fitful sleep at shortly after two o'clock in the morning by a shrill, sibilant, faceless voice that was sitting in my rocking chair. I couldn't make it out at first in the dark bedroom. I said: "I'm sorry, you'll have to talk a little louder." And the Voice said to me: "I want you to tell the people the truth, not an easy thing to do; because the people don't want to know the truth." I said, "You're kidding. How the hell would I know what the truth is?" I mean, you have to picture me sitting there on the foot of the bed, talking to an empty rocking chair. I said to myself, "Howard, you are some kind of banjo-brain, sitting here talking to an empty chair." But the Voice said to me, "Don't worry about the truth. I'll put the words in your mouth." And I said, "What is this, the burning bush? For God's sake, I'm not Moses." And the Voice said to me, "And I'm not God, what's that got to do with it?" And the Voice said to me, "We're not talking about eternal truth or absolute truth or ultimate truth! We're talking about impermanent, transient, human truth! I don't expect you people to be capable of truth! But, goddamit, you're at least capable of self-preservation! That's good enough! I want you to go out and tell the people to preserve themselves." And I said to the Voice, "Why me?" And the Voice said, "Because you're on television, dummy! You have forty million Americans listening to you; after tonight's show, you could have fifty million. For Pete's sake, I don't expect you to walk the land in sackcloth and ashes, preaching the Armageddon. You're on TV, man!" So I thought about it for a moment—and then I said, "Okay."

GO TO YOUR WINDOW AND SHOUT

Bare in mind that in 1976, when this film was released, the following rant rang true with many moviegoers.

Howard: I don't have to tell you things are bad. Everybody knows things are bad. It's a depression. Everybody's out of work or scared of losing their job, the dollar buys a nickel's worth, banks are going bust, shopkeepers keep a gun under the counter, punks are running wild in the streets, and there's nobody anywhere who seems to know what to do, and there's no end to it. We know the air's unfit to breathe and our food is unfit to eat, and we sit and watch our TVs while some local newscaster tells us today we had fifteen homicides and sixty-three violent crimes, as if that's the way it's supposed to be. We all know things are bad. Worse than bad. They're crazy. It's like everything's going crazy. So we don't go out any more. We sit in the house, and slowly the world we live in gets smaller, and all we ask is please, at least leave us alone in our own living rooms. Let me have my toaster and my TV and my hair-dryer and my steel-belted radials, and I won't say anything, just leave us alone. Well, I'm not going to leave you alone. I want you to get mad—I don't want you to riot. I don't want you to protest. I don't want you to write your congressmen. Because I wouldn't know what to tell you to write. I don't know what to do about the depression and the inflation and the defense budget and the Russians and crime in the street. All I know is first you got to get mad. You've got to say: "I'm mad as hell and I'm not going to take this any more. I'm a human being, goddamnit. My life has value." So I want you to get up now. I want you to get out of your chairs and go to the window. Right now. I want you to go to the window, open it, and stick your head out and yell. I want you to yell, "I'm mad as hell and I'm not going to take this any more!" Get up from your chairs. Go to the window. Open it. Stick your head out and yell and keep yelling.—We'll figure out what to do about the depression—and the inflation and the oil crisis. Things have got to change. But you can't change them unless you're mad. You have to get mad. Go to the window. Stick your head out and yell. I want you to yell, "I'm mad as hell and I'm not going to take this any more!" Right now. Get up. Go to your window—Open your window . . .

TURN YOUR TV OFF

And the people did. But Howard, whose rantings have sent his ratings soaring and saved his job, is hardly finished.

Howard: Edward George Ruddy died today! Edward George Ruddy was the Chairman of the Board of the Union Broadcasting Systems—and woe is us if it ever falls in the hands of the wrong people. And that's why woe is us that Edward George Ruddy died. Because this network is now in the hands of CC and A, the Communications Corporation of America. We've got a new Chairman of the Board, a man named Frank Hackett, now sitting in Mr. Ruddy's office on the twentieth floor. And when the twelfth largest company in the world controls the most awesome goddamned propaganda force in the whole godless world, who knows what shit will be peddled for truth on this tube? So listen to me! Television is not the truth! Television is a goddamned amusement park, that's what television is! Television is a circus, a carnival, a travelling troupe of acrobats and storytellers, singers and dancers, jugglers, sideshow freaks, lion tamers and football players. We're in the boredom-killing business! If you want truth, go to God, go to your guru, go to yourself, because that's the only place you'll ever find any real truth! But, man, you're never going to get any truth from us. We'll tell you anything you want to hear. We lie like hell! We'll tell you Kojak always gets the killer, and nobody ever gets cancer in Archie Bunker's house. And no matter how much trouble the hero is in, don't worry: just look at your watch—at the end of the hour he's going to win. We'll tell you any shit you want to hear! We deal in illusion, man! None of it's true! But you people sit there—all of you—day after day, night after night, all ages, colors, creeds—we're all you know. You're beginning to believe this illusion we're spinning here. You're beginning to think the tube is reality and your own lives are unreal. You do whatever the tube tells you. You dress like the tube, you eat like the tube, you raise your children like the tube, you think like the tube. This is mass madness, you maniacs! In God's name, you people are the real thing! We're the illusions! So turn off this goddamn set! Turn it off right now! Turn it off and leave it off. Turn it off right now, right in the middle of this very sentence I'm speaking now—

STOP CC AND A

But Howard's audience rejects his advice.

Howard: All right, listen to me! Listen carefully! This is your goddamn life I'm talking about today! In this country, when one company takes over another company, they simply buy up a controlling share of the stock. But first they have to file notice with the government. That's how CC and A—the Communications Corporation of America—bought up the company that owns this network. And now somebody's buying up CC and A! Some company named Western World Funding Corporation is buying up CC and A! They filed their notice this morning! Well, just who the hell is Western World Funding Corporation? It's a consortium of banks and insurance companies who are not buying CC and A for themselves, but as agents for somebody else! Well, who's this somebody else? They won't tell you! They won't tell you, they won't tell the Senate, they won't tell the SEC, the FCC, the Justice Department, they won't tell anybody! They say it's none of our business! The hell it ain't! Well, I'll tell you who they're buying CC and A for. They're buying it for the Saudi Arabian Investment Corporation! They're buying it for the Arabs! We know the Arabs control more than sixteen billion dollars in this country! They own a chunk of Fifth Avenue, twenty downtown pieces of Boston, a part of the port of New Orleans, an industrial park in Salt Lake City. They own big hunks of the Atlanta Hilton, the Arizona Land and Cattle Company, the Security National Bank in California, the Bank of the Commonwealth in Detroit! They control ARAMCO, so that puts them into Exxon, Texaco and Mobil Oil! They're all over—New Jersey, Louisville, St. Louis, Missouri! And that's only what we know about! There's a hell of a lot more we don't know about, because all those Arab petro-dollars are washed through Switzerland and Canada and the biggest banks in this country! For example, what we don't know about is this CCA deal and all the other CCA deals! Right now, the Arabs have screwed us out of enough American dollars to come back and, with our own money, buy General Motors, IBM, ITT, AT&T, Dupont, U.S. Steel, and twenty other top American companies. Hell, they already own half of England. Now listen to me, goddammit! The Arabs are simply buying us! They're buying all our land, our whole economy, the press, the factories, financial institutions, the government! They're going to own us! A handful of agas, shahs and emirs who despise this country and everything it stands for—democracy, freedom, the right for me to get up on television and tell you about it—a couple of dozen medieval fanatics are going to own where you work, where you live, what you read, what you see, your cars, your bowling alleys, your mortgages, your schools, your churches, your libraries, your kids, your whole life! And there's not a single law on the books to stop them! There's only one thing that can stop them—you! So I want you to get up now. I want you to get out of your chairs and go to the phone. Right now. I want you to go to your phone, or get in your car and drive into the Western Union office in town. I want everybody listening to me to get up right now and send a telegram to the White House. By midnight tonight, I want a million telegrams in the White House! I want them wading knee-deep in telegrams at the White House! Get up! Right now! And send President Ford a telegram, saying: "I'm mad as hell and I'm not going to take this any more! I don't want the banks selling my country to the Arabs! I want this CC and A deal stopped now! I want this CC and A deal stopped now! I want this CC and A deal stopped now!"

THE CORPORATE SOCIETY

And it was.

Howard: Last night, I got up here and asked you people to stand up and fight for your heritage, and you did and it was beautiful. Six million telegrams were received at the White House. The Arab takeover of CC and A has been stopped. The people spoke, the people won. It was a radiant eruption of democracy. But I think that was it, fellers. That sort of thing isn't likely to happen again. Because, in the bottom of all our terrified souls, we all know that democracy is a dying giant, a sick, sick, dying, decaying political concept, writhing in its final pain. I don't mean the United States is finished as a world power. The United States is the most powerful, the richest, the most advanced country in the world, light years ahead of any other country. And I don't mean the communists are going to take over the world. The communists are deader than we are. What's finished is the idea that this great country is dedicated to the freedom and flourishing of every individual in it. It's the individual that's finished. It's the single, solitary human being who's finished. It's every single one of you out there who's finished. Because this is no longer a nation of independent individuals. This is a nation of two hundred- odd million transistorized, deodorized, whiter-than-white, steel-belted bodies, totally unnecessary as human beings and as replaceable as piston rods—Well, the time has come to say: is dehumanization such a bad word? Because, good or bad, that's what's so. The whole world is becoming humanoid, creatures that look human but aren't. The whole world, not just us. We're just the most advanced country, so we're getting there first—The whole world's people are becoming mass-produced, programmed, wired, insensate things useful only to produce and consume other mass-produced things, all of them as unnecessary and useless as we are—that's the simple truth you have to grasp, that human existence is an utterly futile and purposeless thing—Because once you've grasped that, then the whole universe becomes orderly and comprehensible—We are right now living in what has to be called a corporate society, a corporate world, a corporate universe. This world quite simply is a vast cosmology of small corporations orbiting around larger corporations who, in turn, revolve around giant corporations—and this whole, endless, ultimate cosmology is expressly designed for the production and consumption of useless things.

THE SYSTEM

When he is finally called on the carpet by the man behind the company, however, he meets his match.

Jensen: I started as a salesman, Mr. Beale. I sold sewing machines and automobile parts, hair brushes and electronic equipment. They say I can sell anything. I'd like to try and sell something to you: Valhalla. Mr. Beale, please sit down—You have meddled with the primal forces of nature, Mr. Beale, and I won't have it. Is that clear?! You think you have merely stopped a business deal—that is not the case! The Arabs have taken billions of dollars out of this country, and now they must put it back. It is ebb

CHAPTER 6: RANTS   107

and flow, tidal gravity, it is ecological balance! You are an old man who thinks in terms of nations and peoples. There are no nations! There are no peoples! There are no Russians. There are no Arabs! There are no third worlds! There is no West! There is only one holistic system of systems, one vast and immense, interwoven, interacting, multivariate, multinational dominion of dollars! Petrodollars, electrodollars, multidollars, reichmarks, rubles, pounds, and shekels! It is the international system of currency that determines the totality of life on this planet! That is the natural order of things today! That is the atomic, subatomic, and galactic structure of things today! And you have meddled with the primal forces of nature, and you will atone! Am I getting through to you, Mr. Beale? You get up on your little twenty-one inch screen, and howl about America and democracy. There is no America. There is no democracy. There is only IBM and ITT and AT&T and DuPont, Dow, Union Carbide and Exxon. Those are the nations of the world today. What do you think the Russians talk about in their councils of state—Karl Marx? They pull out their linear programming charts, statistical decision theories, and minimax solutions, and compute the price-cost probabilities of their transactions and investments just like we do. We no longer live in a world of nations and ideologies, Mr. Beale. The world is a college of corporations, inexorably determined by the immutable bylaws of business. The world is a business, Mr. Beale! It has been since man crawled out of the slime, and our children, Mr. Beale, will live to see that perfect world in which there is no war and famine, oppression and brutality—one vast and ecumenical holding company, for whom all men will work to serve a common profit, in which all men will hold a share of stock, all necessities provided, all anxieties tranquilized, all boredom amused. And I have chosen you to preach this evangel, Mr. Beale.

Howard: Why me?

Jensen: Because you're on television, dummy.

CHAPTER 7:

Issues

THE WELFARE AND PROGRESS OF MANKIND

After a struggle to win acceptance of his ideas (pasteurization), the great doctor advises his own students in The Story of Louis Pasteur.

Pasteur: You young men—doctors and scientists of the future—do not let yourselves be tainted by a barren skepticism, nor discouraged by the sadness of certain hours that creep over nations. Do not become angry at your opponents, for no scientific theory has ever been accepted without opposition. Live in the serene peace of libraries and laboratories. Say to yourselves first, "What have I done for my instruction?", and, as you gradually advance, "What am I accomplishing?" Until the time comes when you may have the immense happiness of thinking that you have contributed in some way to the welfare and progress of mankind.

THE SMELL OF MY BOOKS

Investigative journalism began with The Life of Emile Zola. *As a young reporter, however, his style wasn't popular with his publisher, who chastises and then fires him for writing "so much muckraking stuff when there are so many pleasant things in life." Zola thanks him for giving him the free time to pursue his own kind of writing.*

Larue: Then go ahead with your scribbling. And maybe a lean stomach will teach you better.

Zola: But a fat stomach sticks out too far, Monsieur Larue. It prevents you from looking down and seeing what is going on around you. While you continue to grow fatter and richer publishing your nauseating confectionery, I shall become a mole digging here, rooting there, stirring up the whole rotten mess where life is hard, raw and ugly! You will not like the smell of my books, Monsieur Larue. Neither will the public prosecutor. But when the stench is strong enough, maybe something will be done about it. Good day.

JUSTICE

Zola's tireless efforts on behalf of army captain Alfred Dreyfuss, a French Jew convicted of treason in a trial tainted by anti-Semitism, help overturn the verdict.

Zola: I feel neither the desire nor the need for triumph. My reward? I have it ever time I think we saved an innocent man from a living death. The thought of seeing him free, of pressing his hands in mine for the first time. That will be reward enough. But our fight is only half won! We must work, my friends, work by speech, by pen, by motion. We of France, who gave the world the boon of liberty, shall we not now give it justice? The very wheels are crying: "Justice! Justice! Justice! Justice!"

I MUST REMEMBER THAT

Successful, Zola is energized for further rabble rousing.

Zola: Ah yes, Dreyfuss! Yes, tomorrow he will be restored to the army . . . You know, it's a queer thing, this Dreyfuss . . . er . . . affair. Before it, I thought my work was done. I could sit back and dream a little. Cezanne was right: I was getting smug and complacent. Then, suddenly, came the Dreyfuss explosion, and I'm alive again. My head bursting with ideas. This new book is bigger than anything I've dared before. The world about to hurl itself to destruction, the will of nations for peace, a powerful brake stopping it on the brink! You don't believe it? Wait! To save Dreyfuss we had to challenge the might of those who dominate the world. It is not the swaggering militarists! They're but puppets that dance as the strings are pulled! It's those others, those who would ruthlessly plunge us into the bloody abyss of war to protect their power. Think of it, Alexandrine, thousands of children sleeping peacefully tonight under the roofs of Paris, Berlin, London, all the world! Doomed to die horribly under some titanic battlefield, unless it can be prevented! And it can be prevented! The world must be conquered, but not by force of arms, but by ideas that liberate. Then can we build it anew, build for the humble and the wretched! That's good! I must remember that.

LIBERTY

When Mr. Smith Goes to Washington, *Washington tries to get the better of him. Undaunted, Smith has other plans.*

Jefferson Smith: I want to make that come to life for every boy in this land. Yes, and lighted up like that too. You see, you see, boys forget what their country means by just reading "the land of the free" in history books. And they get to be men and forget even more. Liberty is too precious to be buried in books, Miss Saunders. Men should hold it up in front of them every single day of their lives, and say: "I am free to think and speak. My ancestors couldn't. I can and my children will." The boys ought to grow up

remembering that. And that, that Steering Committee or whatever it is, they've got to see it like that. And I know Senator Paine will do all he can to help me because he's a wonderful man, isn't he, Miss Saunders? You know, he knew my father very well.

GREAT TRUTHS

Things go against him, but he calls on Americans to help out.

Jefferson Smith: Just get up off the ground. That's all I ask. Get up there with that lady that's up on top of this Capitol dome. That lady that stands for liberty. Take a look at this country through her eyes if you really want to see something. And you won't just see scenery. You'll see the whole parade of what man's carved out for himself after centuries of fighting. And fighting for something better than just jungle law. Fighting so he can stand on his own two feet, free and decent. Like it was created. No matter what his race, color or creed. That's what you'd see. There's no place out there for graft or greed or lies. Or compromise with human liberties.

If that's what the grownups have done with this world that was given to them, then we'd better get those boys camps started fast and see what the kids can do. And it's not too late. Because this country is bigger than the Taylors or you or me or anything else. Great principles don't get lost once they come to light. They are right here. You just have to see them again.

DEAD RIGHT OR CRAZY

Finally, on the floor of the Senate, he makes his point.

Jefferson Smith: "We hold these truths to be self-evident, that all men are created equal, that they are endowed by their Creator with certain unalienable Rights—that among these are life, liberty and the pursuit of Happiness. That to secure these rights, Governments are instituted among Men, deriving their just powers from the consent of the governed, that whenever any form of government becomes destructive of these ends, it is the right of the People to alter or to abolish it, and to institute new government, laying its foundation on such principles and organizing its powers in such form as to them shall seem most likely to effect their Safety and Happiness." Now that's pretty swell, isn't it? I always get such a kick outta those parts of the Declaration—especially when I can read 'em out loud to somebody. You see, that's what I had in mind about camp—except those men said it a little better than I can. Now, you're not gonna have a country that makes these kind of rules work, if you haven't got men who've learned to tell human rights from a punch in the nose. And funny thing about men—they start life being boys. That's why it seemed like a pretty good idea to take kids out of crowded cities and stuffy basements for a few months a year—and build their bodies and minds for a man-sized job. Those boys'll be sitting at these desks some day. Yes—it seemed a pretty good idea—boys coming together—all nationalities and ways of living— finding out what makes different people tick the way they do. 'Cause I wouldn't give you a red cent for all your fine rules, without there was some plain everyday, common kindness under 'em—and a little looking-out for the next fella. Yes—pretty important, all that. Just happens to be blood and bone and sinew of this democracy that some great man handed down to the human race! That's all! But of course, if you need to build a dam where a camp like that ought to be—to make some graft and pay off your political army or something—why, that's different! No sir! If anybody here thinks I'm going back to those boys and say to 'em: "Forget it, fellas. Everything I've told you about the land you live in is a lotta hooey. It isn't your country—it belongs to the James Taylors!" No sir, anybody that thinks that has got another thing coming! I . . . I'm sorry to be coming back to that and—I'm sorry I have to stand here—it's pretty disrespectful to this honorable body. When I think—this was where Clay and Calhoun and Webster spoke—Webster stood right here by this desk—why, nobody like me ought to get in here, in the first place—an' I hate to go on trying your patience like this—but—well, I'm either dead right or I'm crazy!

THEY'RE HUNGRY

Believe it or not, in the late nineteen-thirties, doctors made house calls, even to the city slums. After successfully delivering a new baby, a young doctor muses on the contradictions of his calling, as his patients Fight for Life.

O'Donnell: They were clean, decent people. Did you notice the flower boxes they had? And that was a fine baby. But what will happen to him now? We can bring their babies safely, but how can we keep them alive? Why keep them alive? We tell our mothers: Give them plenty of milk to drink. We say: Feed them cod-liver oil, and orange juice and green vegetables. We say: Keep them clean, and dress them warmly to fight off influenza and pneumonia. We teach them: The sun will make them strong against rickets and help fight T.B. But where do we tell them to go for green vegetables? Where do we tell them to move for the sunshine? We say: Guard against measles and whooping cough and scarlet fever and diphtheria. We tell them: We have science to keep your children from being deaf or blind or crippled for life. But where can we tell them to go for the doctors and the science? There is a house in America . . . They brought them into all our great cities from the hills and fields to build their machines and roll their steel . . . and left them in these shacks. Here are bad teeth and tainted blood and infected lungs. Here are damaged kidneys and cracked hearts and twisted legs. But here are men who want decent clothes and homes and medical care for their women and children. How can they keep alive in these places? Here in these markets and warehouses are millions of pounds of surplus food. Yet there are children in this city who never in their lifetime have eaten a decent meal. We tell them: "Eat liver," and mark anemia on the record . . . We tell them: "Rest in bed," and mark cardiac trouble on the record. We tell them: "Eat fresh vegetables," and mark malnutrition on the record. Why don't we just mark on the record, "They're hungry."

FREE ENTERPRISE

Preston Tucker wanted to build a car that would revolutionize the automotive industry. True story. Naturally, the industry's Big Three conspire to destroy him. Here's Tucker: The Man and His Dream.

Tucker: When I was a boy, I used to read all about Edison and the—Wright Brothers—Mr. Ford they were my heroes. Rags to riches: that's not just the name of a book, that's what this country was all about. We invented the free enterprise system where anybody—no matter who he was, where he came from, what class he belonged to—if he came up with a better idea about anything, there was no limit to how far he could go. I grew up a generation too late, I guess, because now the way the system works, the loner, the dreamer, the crackpot who comes up with some crazy idea that everybody laughs at later, turns out to revolutionize the world—he's squashed from above before he even gets his head out of the water, because the bureaucrats, they'd rather kill a new idea than let it rock the boat. If Benjamin Franklin were alive today, he'd be thrown in jail for sailing a kite without a license! It's true. We're all puffed-up with ourselves now because we invented the Bomb—beat the daylights out of the Japanese, the Nazis. But if big business closes the door on the little guy with the new idea, we're not only closing the door on progress, but we're sabotaging everything that we've fought for. Everything that the country stands for! And one day we're going to find ourselves at the bottom of the heap, instead of king of the hill, having no idea how we got there: buying our radios and our cars from our former enemies. I don't believe that's going to happen—I can't believe it, because if I ever stop believing the plain old common horse sense of the American people, there's no way I could get out of bed in the morning. Thank you.

INTEGRITY LOST AND FOUND

A brief speech about the corrupting influence of being inside the Washington beltway, by a man who once was one of All the President's Men *and now wants to escape.*

Sloan: I wish I could put down on paper what it's like—you come to Washington because you believe in something, and then you get inside and you see how things work, and you watch your ideals disintegrate. The people inside, the people in the White House, they start to believe they can suspend the rules because they're fulfilling a mission. That becomes the only important thing—the mission. It's so easy to lose perspective. We want to get out before we lose ours altogether.

RIGHT VS. WRONG

Davy Crockett, bear hunter, Indian fighter, frontiersman, Tennessee Legislator, and U.S. congressman, met his Maker at The Alamo. *According to John Wayne, it was the right thing to do.*

Davy Crockett: I'm gonna tell you something, Flaca, and I want you to listen tight. May sound like I'm talkin' about me. But I'm not. I'm talkin' about you. As a matter of fact, I'm talkin' about all people everywhere. When I come down here to Texas, I was lookin' for something. I didn't know what. Seems like you added up my life and I spent it all either stompin' other men or, in some cases, gettin' stomped. Had me some money and had me some medals. But none of it seemed worth a lifetime of the pain of the mother that bore me. It was like I was empty. Well, I'm not empty any more. That's what's important. I feel useful in this old world. To hit a lick against what's wrong, or say a word for what's right, even though you get walloped for sayin' that word. Now, I may sound like a bible beater yelling up a revival at a river crossing camp meeting, but that don't change the truth none. There's right and there's wrong. You gotta do one or the other. You do the one, and you're living. You do the other, and you may be walkin' around, but you're dead as a beaver hat.

CHAPTER 8:

Stories

1,000 STORIES

There's a thousand stories in The Naked City. *This detective finds they all have something in common.*

Mulvey: People get so pounded and pounded in this life. It's a jungle, a city like this. Eight million people struggling for life, for food, for air, for a bit of happiness. Seems like there ain't enough of everything to go around . . . and so sometimes it breaks out in . . . violence . . . an' we call it "homicide."

THE COW STORY

Writers love to get in a good joke. Here's a classic from Bonnie and Clyde.

Buck: And the doc, he takes him aside, says, "Son, your old mama just gettin' weak and sickly layin' there. I want you to persuade her to take a little brandy, y'know, to pick her spirits up." "Why, Doc," he says, "you know my mamma is a teetotaler. She wouldn't touch a drop." "Well, I tell you what," the doc says, "why don't you bring her a fresh quart of milk every day from your farm, 'cept you fix it up so half of it's brandy, and don't let on!" So he does that, doctors it up with brandy, and his mamma drinks some of it. And the next day he brings it again, and she drinks some more—and she keeps it up every day. Finally, one week later, he brings her the milk and, don't you know, she just swallows it all down, and looks at her boy and says, "Son, whatever you do, *don't sell that cow!*"

I SHOT AN ELEPHANT IN MY PAJAMAS

Bert Kalmar, George S. Kaufman, Harry Ruby and Morrie Ryskind weren't the Marx Brothers, *but they were* Animal Crackers, *and the best to write for the brilliant comedians.*

Captain Spaulding: Friends, I'm going to tell you of the great, mysterious, wonderful continent known as Africa. Africa, God's country. And he can have it . . . Well, sir, we left New York drunk and early on the morning of February second. After fifteen days on the water and six on the boat we finally arrived on the shores of Africa. We at once proceeded 300 miles into the heart of the jungle, where I shot a polar bear. This bear was 6 foot 7 in his stockinged feet and had shoes on. This bear was anemic and couldn't stand the cold climate. He was a rich bear and could afford to go away in the winter. From the day of our arrival, we led an active life. The first morning saw us up at six, breakfasted, then back in bed at seven. This was our routine for the first three months. We finally got so we were back in bed at six-thirty. One morning I was sitting in front of the cabin, smoking some meat. There wasn't a cigar store in the neighborhood. As I say, I was sitting in front of the cabin when I bagged six tigers. I bagged them, I bagged them to go away, but they hung around all afternoon. They were the most persistent tigers I've ever seen. The principal animals inhabiting the African jungle are moose, elk and Knights of Pythias. Of course you all know what a moose is, that's big game. The first day I shot two bucks—that was the biggest game we had. As I say, you all know what a moose is? A moose runs around on the floor and eats cheese and is chased by the cats. The elks, on the other hand, live up in the hills, and in the spring they come down for their annual convention. It is very interesting to watch them come down to the waterhole. And you should see them run when they find it is only a waterhole. What they're looking for is an elk-a-hole. One morning I shot an elephant in my pajamas. How he got in my pajamas, I'll never know. But that is entirely irrelevant to what I was talking about. We took some pictures of the native girls, but they weren't developed. But we're going back again in a couple of weeks . . .

CHAPTER 9:

Hollywood

THE OUTSIDER

Paddy Chayefsky had a lot to say, especially about Hollywood. Here a poor, small town teenage girl, soon to become The Goddess *of Hollywood, feels sorry for herself, and wants her date to know it.*

Emily Ann: I didn't exactly have a case on you myself, but I was very pleased when you asked me to go out with you today. I'm well aware that your daddy is a doctor and that there are many people in this city who look upon my mother and myself as common. Well, before my daddy died, we lived in Clarksville, Tennessee, and my father had the dry cleaning store, and we were well thought of. My mother had a nigger come in twice a week to help her with the washing and ironing. We were one of the better families. There's lots of girls here wish they had my background. I know I don't get invited to the Cotillion and the Subdeb, and you don't know how that hurt me! I cried for weeks! I could have killed Thelma Doris and her mother. Supposed to be my friend. Didn't even invite me to her sweet sixteen party. I begged my mother a hundred times—let's move out of niggertown. But she's crazy about money. She hoards it away. I don't even know where, myself. She don't want to pay more than seven dollars a month for that tacky little old three rooms we got there. What do you think I work in Rice's five-and-dime after school for? She won't give me a penny to buy new clothes! I have to buy all my own clothes. I even saved up and bought my own public school graduation dress, the material, and sewed it myself. Everybody thought it was beautiful. They thought I'd gone to Baltimore to get it! Well, I certainly have a temper, don't I? I apologize, Lewis, for that outburst, but I feel these things very deeply. I don't expect you can understand the shame and degradation that a girl feels when she isn't invited to a sweet sixteen party.

MOVIE STARS

But she has big dreams.

Emily Ann: Her real name isn't Ginger Rogers, you know. Her real name is Virginia McMath, and you know how she got started? She used to dance in Charleston contests, and somebody saw her, and that's how she become a star. I was thinking of taking dancing lessons, tap dancing and things like that, but they don't even have any place there in Hagerstown where they teach that. Do you know of any? Lana Turner was discovered in a drug store, and there was one star—I think it was Priscilla Lane or Carole Landis—was just an old secretary, and she was riding up in the elevator, and this producer saw her and that's how she got her start. But I was talking about Ginger Rogers. I mean, she ain't like some of them stars. She don't go out to nightclubs much, although there was one time there everybody thought she was going to marry Howard Hughes—it was in all the magazines. Anyway, she lives in a lovely home in Beverly Hills with her mother. She keeps her mother right there with her. I think that's nice. Ginger Rogers' dressing room has mirrors on the ceiling and the walls, and she has fruitwood furniture, and she loves classical music, you know? She's very close with Deems Taylor. He's a well-known classical musician. She has his picture on the wall but there's no romance there in the wind, I don't think—just good friends. Where are you going, Lewis?

A MOVIE STAR'S SON

Later, she attaches herself to a movie star's son. He explains himself.

Tower: Don't leave me now. I won't do anything terrible except possibly commit suicide. That's what I came up here for, you know. Drown myself in the bathtub. Go look in there. The bath is full. I got blind as a coot last night and staggered in stark naked, and fell in the tub and put my head under the water, and I almost did it. I can't describe to you the absolute tranquility. But way back in the empty hollow some persistent hammer of life clunked away, and, at the last minute, I pulled my head up and gasped in the air, and I lay on the dirty, cold wet tiles twitching like a fish in the bottom of a boat. I just don't have the talent for suicide. I took seventeen sleeping pills in the Ashford Hotel in New York, but they rushed up the stairs with a stomach pump, and I spent the night in Bellevue. I tried gas, but all I got was color in my cheeks. I just don't have the knack. What are you living for? Be honest now. Tell me. What's it going to add up to, this sixty, seventy years you're going to flounder around this earth? One day you'll be necking in the back of the car with one of the boys from town, and because all your friends are getting married, you'll get married. You'll put on weight, and your husband will take up with a waitress in a hotel in Chattanooga. You'll have babies and visit your in-laws in the evening, and your husband will get sick, and you'll fret about the rent. Your hair will gray, and you'll suddenly look back and say, "What happened? It's all over." Your friends will die and you'll sink into melancholic hours, sitting by a window, peering with unseeing eyes through white chintz curtains, and finally they'll drop your long wooden box into the moldering grave. And what was it all about except worry and tears? Am I lying? Isn't that it? Slings and arrows. A tale told by an idiot. Why bother? It all ends up in the grave. You might as well make an honest effort to get there . . . What would you know about it anyway, a frump in a hick town? You don't know what loneliness is. You think it's not having a date on Saturday night. You don't know the great, ultimate ache of desolation. I'm cold. Close the window or something . . . The last time I saw my father was six years ago. He was sitting in the living room of that barn he has in Sherman Oaks, playing solitaire, guzzling wine because he's too miser-cheap to buy a decent fifth of Irish whisky, half hidden behind a thin blanket of cigarette smoke. The house was empty. My mother had a nervous breakdown when I was eleven. My older brother, Tom—my old man drove him years ago into an insane asylum, where he walks around picking up imaginary strings off the floor. My father said, "Where have you been the last couple of weeks?" Last couple of weeks! I had been gone for a year and a half in the Spanish Civil War. I said, "Pa, I need psychiatric help. I'm lost. I have to fight sometimes to keep myself from jumping out of windows. I'm asking you to be kind to me." He said, "I'm supporting one crazy son and that's enough for me." That's my old man, star of stage, screen and radio, and a host of favorite . . . You wouldn't understand, you wouldn't understand. You don't know what loneliness means. All you ever cried at was a Street and Smith love story.

A CHILDHOOD IN BOOKS

And talks about his childhood.

Tower: When I was twelve years old, I was in Andover prep school. Very fancy. My father sent me to one fancy boarding school after another. I got thrown out of all of them. But when I was in Andover I knew a boy—we shared a room together—a blond boy named Elliot Sherman, and we used to sit up all night long talking about everything. He was the only boy I ever met who had read as much as I had. You can't imagine what I had read by the time I was twelve. My father had thousands and thousands of books. He bought this huge shack out in Sherman Oaks, California, and the library came with it. He never read a one of them; I read them all. Lucretius and Sophocles—all the great, desolate dramas of antiquity. I wore out Shakespeare and Macaulay and Gibbon, the fat sprawling histories of the Victorians, obscure poetry by B.V. Thompson and the elegant jaded sensuality of the Pre-Raphaelites. I used to lie all alone in the bleak, shadowed living room and read until my head fell on the books. Mark Twain. I adored him. That's all I own now are a few slim volumes of Mark Twain's black little pessimism, *Pudd'nhead Wilson's Notebook What Is Man?*, and a collection of Eugene O'Neill, that great Irish peddler of death. I was twelve years old, mind you, and I used to stand in that empty living room quoting the sonorous despair of Edwin Arlington Robinson and the biting contempt of Jeffers. My father was out chasing some tart, and my sixteen-year-old brother was out wandering the streets, half demented. What a family, huh? Well, anyway, there was this boy in Andover when I was twelve years old, and we used to talk all night long. And to this day, you're the only other person I've ever talked with like that.

THE STARLET

In Hollywood at last, Emily Ann Faulkner (now Rita Shawn) meets a genuine starlet.

Joanna: When I was eight years old, I won the Prettiest Child at the Missouri State Country Fair, and that's all my mother had to hear. She whisked me up to New York, and she had me taking ballet lessons at Carnegie Hall. Whole bunch of us little girls prancing around on our skinny legs. She had me modeling for John Robert Powers when I was fifteen years old. I made eleven thousand dollars when I was fifteen years old. Well, I been out here eleven years now, and it's about time she realizes she ain't never going to be the mother of a big movie star. If you don't make it by the time you're twenty-eight, you never make it. I'm taking extra calls now, standing on line, making eyes at some assistant director. I don't know how to get out of this, don't you understand? I don't know where to go. I keep dreaming I'll meet some man who will marry me and take me away. Who, Eddie Rogers? I been going with him for four months and I don't even like him. He's a vicious drunk; I never know what he's going to do. And after him somebody just like him. I wish I could just go to sleep and sleep and sleep.

HER HERITAGE

Having pulled himself together, the movie star's son brings their daughter to visit his ex-wife, the movie star.

Tower: Miss Haywood, this is none of your business. It is your job, Miss Haywood, to hover over that poor desolate woman upstairs. My job is to give my daughter some love of life. I don't really care about Rita Shawn any more. Or myself. We are a gutted generation, born in the depression and obsessed with prosperity. Well, we got prosperity, and what have we got? A hysterical woman upstairs who needs barbiturates to put her to sleep, Dexedrine Spansules to wake her up, and tranquilizers to keep her numb, who has a nervous breakdown once a year and has tried to kill herself at least four times that the public knows. I don't want my daughter to grow up like that. Or like me. A twisted, loveless man, patched together by psychoanalysis. My daughter was a very strange little girl for a long time, well on her way to continuing the desolate pattern of her parents, her grandparents, and all the generations before her, the long parade of history that has brought us to this year of suicide and insanity. Do you think I would take this frightened little girl and send her for two weeks with a meaningless mother, to be devoured by this wandering panther of a woman as she prowls through life looking for some reason for living? My daughter has a reason for living. She's not going to scream out in a hot cemetery that she wants to die. She wants to see her mother very much. She is a sweet girl. She has given me the little importance in life that I have. I thought she might give Rita a little of that.

WHAT IT TAKES TO BE A MOVIE STAR

An American movie star (Julia Roberts—playing Julia Roberts) lets her hair down before the denizens of Notting Hill.

Anna: Well, I've been on a diet since I was nineteen, which means basically I've been hungry for a decade. I've had a sequence of not-nice boyfriends—one of whom hit me—and every time my heart gets broken, it gets splashed across the newspapers as entertainment. Meantime, it cost millions to get me looking like this, and one day, not long from now, my looks will go, they'll find out I can't act, and I'll become a sad middle-aged woman who looks a bit like someone who was famous for a while.

THE HEADLESS HORSEMAN

In Curse of the Cat People, *an aging actress relates the Legend of the Headless Horseman. A metaphor?*

Julia Farren: On the dark nights, on the stormy nights, you can hear him. He passes like the wind, and the flapping and fluttering of his great cloak, beating like gaunt wings, and the thunder of his horses' hooves is loud . . . and loud . . . and louder! At the midnight hour, down the road that leads to Sleepy Hollow, across the bridge, he goes galloping, galloping, galloping, always searching, always seeking. And if you stand on the bridge at the wrong hour, the hour when he rides by, his great cloak sweeps 'round you! He swings you to his saddle-bow, and then forever you must ride. And always his cold arms around you, clasping you into the cavity of his bony chest. And then, forever, you must ride, and ride, and ride—with the Headless Horseman.

A STORY IDEA

What Price Hollywood? You have to listen to producers like this one to know.

Saxe: Wait a minute. I got an idea. We'll throw the whole thing out the window. I got a story of my own. It's my own brainchild. I had it in the back of my head for fifteen years. It probably won't make a dime, but it's an artistic triumph. It's about an old general. In Russia. It's the night of the grand ball. Splashes of color. Music. Jewels. Throbbing pulses. They are dancing a minuet. The old general is stooped, and he carries a long cane as he dance with the duchess. Nobody would know he was the famous general of all Russia. Then, suddenly, a messenger throws open the door. He calls out, as he holds a document: "A letter from the Czarina." The music stops. The general reads the letter. He takes his cane like a sword. He is not stooped now. He is the great general who left behind . . . I forgot to tell you . . . because he is too old. I told the ending first, it was too dramatic. Never mind. He takes his cane and gives orders: "You go to Greece." "You take charge of the Turkish front." "You do this" and "you do that." How does it sound so far?

THE MOVIE EXECUTIVE

A modern film executive regards himself as The Player. *He tells us why writers hate studio execs.*

Griffin Mill: Well, I listen to stories and decide if they'll make good movies or not. I get 125 phone calls a day, and if I let that slip to 100, I know I'm not doing my job. Everyone that calls, they want to know one thing: They want me to say "yes" to them and make their movie. If I say "yes" to them, and make their movie, they think that, come next New Year's it's going to be them and Jack Nicholson on the slopes of Aspen. That's what they think. Problem is, I can only say "yes," my studio can only say "yes," twelve times a year, and collectively we hear about 50,000 stories a year. So it's hard, and I guess sometimes I'm not nice and I make enemies, and that's what I was to David, an enemy. His story lacked certain elements we need to market a film successfully—suspense, laughter, violence, hope, heart, nudity, sex, happy endings. Mainly happy endings.

THE IDEALIST

Hollywood is full of The Bad and the Beautiful, *including this cynical bit player from Europe.*

Rosa: Ach! You don't even know the difference between a performance and a personality. Here in Hollywood you are all the same. Directors, producers, cameramen. All you care about is sex, sex, sex, sex—and ballyhoo. Technique, you have—great technique—and what do you use it for? To reveal the soul? To cut into the heart? To tell the truth? No! The greatest technique in the world—and how do you use it? For horses, or close-ups! Close-ups of tailor's dummies and fashion models. How do you reveal the soul? How do you cut into the heart? Your films are like your bathrooms—beautiful, shiny, stainless, antiseptic—and empty.

THE PRODUCER

In Hollywood, everyone is Swimming with Sharks. *Here is a film producer explaining, as he reams out his young assistant, why he's an asshole.*

Buddy Ackerman: Christmas Eve. Twelve years ago. She was on her way to the mall. I was supposed to have gone with her. We hadn't started our Christmas shopping yet. But it was gonna be simple. Just some stuff for our parents. Money was tight and shopping was a hassle, anyway. We even promised not to give each other gifts. On the way there was a car that had broken down, so Mallory pulled over to help. I always told her she was such a busybody, but she just called it being nice. She got out and asked if everything was all right, or something stupid. Anyway, it was a scam. Bunch of punk kids stealing cars. They shot her. I was stuck at the office, wrapping Christmas gifts for my boss. Lot of gifts. We'd had a good year that year. I was there till three a.m. And the whole time I'm thinking to myself, "Oh boy. She is gonna be pissed. When I get home, I am a dead man." Anyway, I got home, got the message, went down to the hospital to identify her. It was a whole week into the New Year before I found them. These stupid wind-up toys and a note: "In the constant rat race of life, don't ever forget to unwind." She was never really any good at writing notes. You think you know it all, don't you? You're 25 years old. You're a baby. You don't know shit. Look, I can appreciate this. I was young, too. I felt just like you. Hated authority. Hated all my bosses, thought they were full of shit. Look, it's like they say: "If you're not a rebel by the age of 20, you got no heart, but if you haven't turned establishment by 30, you've got no brains!" Because there are no storybook romances, no fairy tale endings. So before you run out and change the world, ask yourself—What do you really want? Don't come preaching to me about your idea of what's fair. Because you're no martyr here. You're no hero. You're just a fucking hypocrite. You're just like any other punk kid out there, looking for a way in, any way in, and you need me. What, you think someone just handed me this job? I've handled the phones. I've juggled the bimbos. I've—I've put up with the tyrants, the yellers, the screamers. I've done more than you can even imagine in that small mind of yours. I've paid my dues—dammit, it's my turn to be selfish. It's my turn. See, that's the trouble with your fucking MTV, microwave-dinner generation. You all want it now. You think you deserve it just because you want it? It doesn't work like that. You have to earn it. You have to take it. You have to make it yours. But first, Guy, you need to decide what it is you really want. You wanna go back to your shitty little existence? Go ahead, leave. There's the door. No one's stopping you. You could have left any day, but you stayed. So let's forget the Dudley-damn-do-right crap. Because out here it's kill your parents, fuck your friends, and have a nice day! Look, I don't make the rules. I play by them. What, your job is unfair to you? Grow up, way it goes. People use you? Life's unfair? Grow up, way it goes. Your girlfriend doesn't love you? Tough shit, way it goes. Your wife gets raped, and shot, and they leave their unfinished beers—their—their stinking long-necks—just lying there on the ground?—So be it. Way it goes.

CHAPTER 10:

The Theatre

JOE GIDEON

You want to know what the show business is really like? Director/choreographer Bob Fosse created an autobiographical film, in which he summed himself, and All That Jazz, *up, with this introduction. (Read in the hep-cat style of Sammy Davis, Jr.)*

O'connor Flood: Folks, what can I tell you about my next guest? This cat allowed himself to be adored, but not loved. Strictly a pro since age thirteen, starting in sleazy Chicago dives and bur-lee-cue, this cat rose to become a leading director-choreographer on the Great White Way and in flicks. But success in showbiz was matched by failure in the personal relationships bag, and from all this experience he came to believe that his whole scene—work, showbiz, personal life, even himself—all that jazz— was bullshit. The cat swung between heavy ego and very heavy self doubt. He had become Numero Uno game player—like to where he didn't know (*doing "Amos and Andy"*). . . wheah de game ended an' de reality began. Like, to him the only reality . . . is death, man. Let me lay on you . . . a so-so entertainer . . . not much of a humanitarian . . . And he was never nobody's friend . . . In his final appearance on the great stage of life . . . Mistuh Joe Gideon.

ON THEATRE

I couldn't resist this short speech from Shakespeare in Love *because of its underlying passion for the ancient art of theatre. When Shakespeare's producer needs a stage, his rival explains why, in this crisis, they will collaborate.*

Burbage: The Master of the Revels despises us for vagrants, tinkers, and peddlers of bombast. But my father, James Burbage, had the first license to make a company of players from Her Majesty, and he drew from poets the literature of the age. Their fame will be our fame. So let them all know, we are men of parts. We are a brotherhood, and we will be a profession. Will Shakespeare has a play. I have a theatre. The Curtain is yours.

ON THEATRE

Another great description of the theatre (which many writers naturally revere) is given to The Elephant Man *by the reigning actress of her day.*

Mrs. Kendal: It's very difficult to put into a nutshell, but I should say the theatre is the shrine of the imagination, where one may suspend disbelief and travel anywhere in the world, to any time you desire. You may look over the shoulders of kings, unobserved, battle with ruthless tyrants, and marry the beautiful princess, all in the space of a few hours. Onstage you may be whoever you wish to be, do anything you please, and always, always live happily ever after. The theatre is all the brightest and best things of the world, Mr. Merrick. It is lights and music, gaiety and joy. It's . . . well, it's romance. That's one thing the theatre has in great store.

I'LL DO IT!

The granddaddy of movie musicals is actually about Broadway musicals. Here's how one was put together in the early days on 42nd Street.

Marsh: You'll get your *Pretty Lady!* YOU haven't got anything to worry about. I'm not going to let you down . . . because I can't afford to! I've given everything I've had to that gulch down there. It's taken all I had to offer. It paid me . . . sure . . . in money I couldn't hang on to. Fair-weather friends, women, headlines. Why, even the cops and newsboys recognize me on eyesight. Marsh, the magnificent. Marsh, the slave driver. Actors tell you how Marsh drove 'em, bullied 'em, and tore it out of them. And maybe a few'll tell you how Marsh really made 'em. And they all have something to show for it . . . except Marsh! Well, this is my last shot! I'll make a few more of 'em, and this time I'll sock my money away so hard they'll have to blast to find enough to buy a newspaper! THAT'S why I'm going ahead with *Pretty Lady!* And that's why *Pretty Lady* has GOT to be a hit. It's my last show—it's GOT to be my best. You're counting on me. Well—I'm counting on *Pretty Lady*. It's got to support ME for a long time to come.

REHEARSALS

And so he begins rehearsals.

Marsh: *All right.*—Now—you people—everybody quiet! And listen to me! Tomorrow morning—we're going to start a show. We're going to rehearse for six weeks and then—We're going to open on schedule time . . . and I *mean* schedule time. You're going to work and sweat and work some more. You're going to work days . . . and you're going to work nights—and you're going to work between times . . . when I think you need it. —You're going to dance until your feet fall off—and you aren't able to stand up. But six weeks from now—we're going to have a SHOW! Now some of you have been with me before, and you know it's going to be a tough grind! It's going to be the toughest six weeks you ever lived through. Do you all get that? Now, anybody who doesn't think he's going to like it had better quit right now! Nobody? Good! Then that's settled. We start tomorrow.

THE STAR STEPS ASIDE

The star gracefully gives way to her understudy.

Dorothy: Listen to me—When I started for here tonight—I was going to tear your heart out. And then I got to thinking . I've had my chance—Now it's your turn. You want fame—well, you'll probably get it. And why not? I've had enough. For five years it's kept me away from the only thing I've ever wanted, and, funny thing, it was a broken ankle that helped me find it out. That's why I'm not burnt up or resentful. A career? Anybody can have one—with the right breaks. As for me—I'll take Pat, and vaudeville, or whatever goes with him. We're being married—tomorrow.

FROM CHORUS TO STAR

Opening night. In perhaps the most famous speech in movie history, the director gives the understudy one last direction.

Marsh: Now listen to me—listen hard. Two hundred people—two hundred jobs—two hundred thousand dollars—five weeks of grind,—and blood and sweat—depend on you. It's the life of all these people who have worked with you. You've got to go on—and you've got to give—and give, and give.—They've GOT to like you,—GOT to—you understand. You can't fall down—you *can't*— Your future's in it—my future's in it—and everything that all of us have is staked on you—I'm through—Now keep your feet on the ground—and your head on those shoulders of yours—and go out—And Sawyer—you're going out a youngster—you've GOT to come back a star! There's your cue!

CHAPTER 11:

Romance

Some simple musings from two Tin Men *who have learned what they know about life by selling aluminum siding door-to-door...*

LIFE IS MORE COMPLICATED TODAY

Some thoughts on relationships...

BB: Look how much more complicated things are now. There used to be a time you met a girl, you courted, and then you got married and lived happily ever after. Now, see that one over there . . . that's Helen Arkon. Maiden name used to be Tudor. Get this, she dated Charlie Rider when I was in high school, seemed like they were together forever. They broke up; she started to go with Lenny Mardigian; they got married; she's Helen Mardigian. That goes on two years, three years, something like that. They divorce, she dates Billy Small for a couple of years, lives with John Bookly for a year, marries Tommy Selnini. That marriage goes in the toilet, but fast. Now she's dating Charlie Rider who was divorced by Evelyn Chartoff, who used to be Evelyn Gage before that. So much for relationships.

BONANZA

And some thoughts on television...

Sam: You know, when I saw "Bonanza" the other day, something occurred to me. There's those four guys living on the Ponderosa, and you never hear them say anything about wanting to get laid. You never hear Hoss turn to Little Joe and say, "I had such a hard-on when I woke up this morning," You know, they never talk about broads . . . nothing. Ya never hear Little Joe say, "Hey, Hoss, I went into Virginia City and saw a girl with the greatest ass I ever saw in my life." Ya just see 'em walking around the Ponderosa saying, "Yes, Pa," and, "Where's Little Joe?" Nothing about broads. I don't think I'm being too picky. At least once if they talked about getting horny. I don't care if you're living on the Ponderosa or right here in Baltimore, guys talk about getting laid. I'm beginning to think that show doesn't have too much realism. What do you think, Tilley?

ROMANCE IS

A rootless radio personality meets a homeless man, learns the legend of The
Fisher King *and this great definition of love.*

Parry: Romance is romance no matter what kind. It could be a Victorian
lady kidnapped by a virile sea captain with a hairy chest, or a horny pizza
boy seduced by a housewife with a hairy upper lip. As long as there's heart,
passion, and a little bit of fantasy. Romance is the stuff of dreams. There's
always more to trash than meets the eye.

PASSION

When death takes a holiday, the billionaire media baron William Parrish gets to Meet Joe Black. *This leads to good advice for his daughter.*

Parrish: I know it's a cornball thing, but love is passion, obsession, someone you can't live without. If you don't start with that, what are you going to end up with? I say fall head over heels. Find someone you can love like crazy and who'll love you the same way back. And how do you find him? Forget your head and listen to your heart. I'm not hearing any heart. (a moment) Run the risk; if you get hurt, you'll come back. Because the truth is there is no sense living your life without this. To make the journey and not fall deeply in love—well, you haven't lived a life at all. You have to try. Because if you haven't tried, you haven't lived.

TOO OLD FOR YOU

A wealthy octogenarian meets a young woman, and regrets that they can't have a relationship. Perhaps that's always The Palm Beach Story.

King: I'd be too old for you . . . cold are the hands of time that creep along relentlessly destroying slowly but without pity that which yesterday was young. Alone our memories resist this disintegration and grow more lovely with the passing years . . . that's hard to say with false teeth.

ANALYZE THIS

More on passion, this time in the form of advice to Ninotchka.

Leon: You analyze everything out of existence. You analyze *me* out of existence. I won't let you. Love is not so simple. Ninotchka, Ninotchka, why do doves bill and coo? Why do snails, coldest of all creatures, circle interminably around each other? Why do moths fly hundreds of miles to find their mates? Why do flowers open their petals? Oh, Ninotchka,

Ninotchka, surely you feel some slight symptom of the divine passion, a general warmth in the palms of your hands, a strange heaviness in your limbs, a burning of the lips that is not thirst but a thousand times more tantalizing, more exalting, than thirst?

I LOVE YOU

Usually, Hollywood he-men are silent types. But to The Lady Eve, *this love struck young man has no problems.*

Charles: I've just understood something . . . You see, every time I've looked at you here on the boat, it wasn't only here I saw you— you seemed to go way back. I know that isn't clear, but I saw you there and at the same time further away, and then still further away, and then very small, like converging perspective lines. No, that isn't it, more like figures following each other in a forest glade. Only way back there you were a little girl in short dresses, with your hair falling on your shoulders . . . in the middle distance your hair is up, but you're still gawky like a colt. Then when you get nearer you look more like you do now, except not so pretty. But I've only told you half of it, because way back there a little boy is standing with you, holding your hand, and in the middle distance I'm still with you, not holding your hand any more because it isn't manly, but wanting to. And then, still nearer, we look terrible: you with your legs like a colt and mine like a calf. What I'm trying to say—only I'm not a poet, I'm an ophiologist— is that I've always loved you. I mean I've never loved anyone but you. I suppose that sounds as dull as a drug store novel, and what I see inside I'll never be able to cast into words, but that's what I mean.

ANOTHER I LOVE YOU

Melvin, a misanthrope whose phobia-filled life is As Good As It Gets, *spends much of his verbal energy insulting people. When Melvin finally finds someone he likes—though it takes him an entire film to realize it—he professes his love as only he can.*

Melvin: Let me just talk. I'm the only one on the face of the earth who realizes that you're the greatest woman on earth. I'm the only one who appreciates how amazing you are in every single thing you do—in every single thought you have. In how you are with Spencer—Spence. In how you say what you mean, and how you almost always mean something that's all about being straight and good. I think most people miss that about you, and I watch, wondering how they can watch you bring them food and clear their dishes and never get that they have just met the greatest woman alive. And the fact that I get it makes me feel great . . . about me! You got a real good reason to walk out on that?

I WOULD LOVE TO FUCK YOU

A different approach is favored by this timeless man.

Darryl Van Horn: Fidel, that's his name. Women love him. They're crazy about him. He has a big *shlong*. Huge. Well, there you are: scale again, size. I don't know, maybe it's a masculine thing. They say women don't care. I'm sort of in the middle myself. How about you? You see, women are in touch with different things. That's my opinion. I know it's not a fashionable opinion right now, but fuck it, I know what I see. I see men running around, trying to put their dicks into everything, trying to make something happen. But it's women who are the source. The only power. Nature. Birth. Rebirth. Cliché, cliché. Sure, but true. I like women. I admire them. But if you want me to treat you like a dumb twit, I will. But what's the point? You have brains, Alex. More than brains, and you don't even know it, do you? Well, most women do not. Where's your husband? When a woman unloads a husband or a husband unloads a woman—however it happens—death, desertion, divorce, the three D's—when that happens a woman blooms. She blossoms, like flowers, like fruit. She is ripe. That's the woman for me. Would you like to see my house? In case anybody ever needs any exercise, the pool's right over there, past the piano where the ballroom used to be. Interesting word, ballroom. And over there is my study. Ah, this is my bedroom. The Borgias once owned the bed. Of course, you have to pay for it with your soul, but what the hell?

I deserve a little luxury. You have to take care of yourself. No one's going to do that for you, are they? I'm being as direct with you as I know how. I thought you might appreciate it. Anyway, I always like a little pussy after lunch. What do you say? Hmmmm? I would never insult your intelligence with something as trivial as seduction. But I would love to fuck you.

HER ANSWER

Unfortunately for him, she's one of The Witches of Eastwick.

Alex: Are you trying to seduce me? Well, I have to admit that I appreciate your directness, Darryl, and I will try to be as direct and honest with you as I possibly can. I think—no, I am positive—that you are the most unattractive man I have ever met in my entire life. You know, in the short time we've been together you have demonstrated every loathsome characteristic of the male personality, and even discovered a few new ones. You are physically repulsive, intellectually retarded, you're morally reprehensible, vulgar, insensitive, selfish, stupid, you have no taste, a lousy sense of humor, and you smell. You're not even interesting enough to make me sick. Goodbye, Darryl, and thank you for a lovely lunch.

WOMEN

Moreover, she and her friends get the better of him—no easy task, as he really is the devil—and send him crashing into a crowded church on a Sunday. His sermon:

Darryl Van Horn: Sorry, just having a little trouble, trouble at home. Little domestic problem. Nothing to be alarmed at, just a little female problem. Ungrateful little bitches, aren't they? May I ask you something? You're all church-going folk. I really want to ask you something. Do you think God knew what he was doing when he created woman? No shit, I really want to know. Or do you think it was another one of his minor mistakes? Like tidal waves, earthquakes, floods. Do you think women are like that? What's the matter? You don't think God makes mistakes? Of course he does! We all make mistakes. Of course, when we make mistakes they call it "evil," when God makes mistakes they call it "nature." So, what do you think? Women: a mistake,— or did He do it to us on purpose? Because I really want to know. Because, if it's a mistake, maybe we can do something about it. Find a cure. Invent a vaccine. Build up our immune systems. Get a little exercise. You know, twenty push-ups a day and you never have to be afflicted with women again. Eat broccoli.

PATRIOTISM AND PROMISCUITY

The Miracle of Morgan's Creek is the birth of sextuplets nine months after a night of debauchery between our heroine and several soldiers heading overseas. This doctor should have warned her sooner.

Doctor Upperman: When the abominations we have committed seem at last to have filled the cup till it overfloweth, when the world is being destroyed, when God seems to have abandoned us to our own miserable devices and the race of men is rapidly vanishing from this earth, it may be particularly appropriate to talk about creation, and particularly creation in wartime, when it is so needful for future wars . . . and God blessed them and God said unto them, "Be fruitful and multiply and replenish the earth . . . and subdue it." Wartime is a dangerous time, not only for the brave young men who sally forth to battle, but also for their fathers and mothers, and for their sisters, particularly for their sisters. It is to these I speak today, to these and to their parents. God said be fruitful and multiply and replenish the earth and it is a fact that during war the earth is more fruitfully replenished than during peace. The uniforms, the brass buttons, the bright colors, the helmets with plumes and horses' tails, the music, all of these have so captured the imagination, electrified the emotions of all young women from the beginning until now, that more little children, little boys especially, are born in war time than any other time, which is excellent in itself, but attended, as are so many excellent things, with dangers. Our homes are surrounded by camps. The camps are full of lonely young men. Let me be the last to speak against them or urge a lack of hospitality, but let me be the first to remind you that all is not gold that glitters, that the young are impetuous, that war time is a thoughtless time and that in any large group of good men there are of necessity some fools and scoundrels . . . and against these I warn you. Beware of the spell cast by jingling spurs, of the hasty act repented at leisure, of confusing patriotism with promiscuity, of interpreting loyalty as laxity. Beware, young women.

WHEN MEN MARRY

When she discovers that she doesn't know whom she drunkenly married, she receives advice that's too little and too late.

Johnson: The responsibility of recording a marriage has always been up to the woman; if it weren't for them, marriage would have disappeared long since. No man is going to jeopardize his present or poison his future with a lot of little brats hollering around the house unless he is forced to. It is up to the woman to knock him down and hog-tie him and drag him in front of two witnesses immediately, if not sooner. Any time after that is too late.

AVAILABLE MEN

A woman feeling The Big Chill *has a thing to say about men.*

Meg: They're either married or gay. And if they're not gay, they've just broken up with the most wonderful woman in the world, or they've just broken up with a bitch who looks exactly like me. They're in transition from a monogamous relationship and they need more space. Or they're tired of space, but they just can't commit. Or they want to commit, but they're afraid to get close. They want to get close, you don't want to get near them.

RELATIONSHIPS

When Harry Met Sally, *they were just good friends. She tells him about a failed relationship that sounds like a lot of failed relationships.*

Sally: When Joe and I first started seeing each other, we wanted exactly the same thing. We wanted to live together, but we didn't want to get married because any time anyone we knew got married, it ruined their relationship. They practically never had sex again. It's true. It's one of the secrets no one ever tells you. I would sit around with my girlfriends who have kids, well, my one girlfriend who has kids, Alice, and she would complain about how she and Gary never did it anymore. She didn't even complain about it, now that I think about it. She just said it matter-of-factly. She said they were up all night, they were both exhausted, the kids just took every sexual impulse out of them. And Joe and I used to talk about it, and we'd say we were so lucky to have this wonderful relationship, we can have sex on the kitchen floor and not worry about the kids walking in; we can fly off to Rome on a moment's notice. And then one day I was taking Alice's little girl for the afternoon because I'd promised her I'd take her to the circus, and we were in the cab playing "I Spy"—I spy a mailbox, I spy a lamppost—and she looked out the window and she saw this man and this woman and these two little kids, and the man had one of the kids on his shoulders, and Alice's little girl said, "I spy a family," and I started to cry. You know, I just started crying. And I went home and I said, "The thing is,

Joe, we never do fly off to Rome on a moment's notice." And that kitchen floor? Not once. It's this very cold, hard Mexican ceramic tile. Anyway, we talked about it for a long time, and I said, this is what I want, and he said, well, I don't, and I said, well, I guess it's over, and he left. And the thing is, I feel fine. I am over him. I mean, I really am over him. That was it for him, that was the most he could give, and every time I think about it, I am more and more convinced that I did the right thing.

PHYSICAL RELATIONSHIPS GET OLD

The truth about Beautiful Girls *from one who isn't...*

Gina: I'm speaking to both of you, okay, you're both fucking insane. You wanna know what your problem is? MTV, Playboy, and Madison fucking Avenue. Yes. Let me explain something to you. OK, look, girls with big tits have big asses, girls with little tits have little asses. That's the way it goes. God doesn't fuck around, he's a fair guy. He gave the fatties big, beautiful tits, and the skinnies little, tiny niddlers. It's not my rule. If you don't like it, call him. Oh guys, look what we have here (*picks up* Penthouse *magazine and opens it*). Look at this, your favorite. Oh, you like that?

Tommy: I'd go along with that.

Gina: Yeah, that's nice, right? Well, it doesn't exist, okay? Look at the hair. The hair is long, it's flowing, it's like a river. Well, it's a fucking weave, okay? And the tits. Please, I could hang my overcoat on them. Tits, by design, were invented to be suckled by babies. Yeah, they're purely functional. These are silicone city. And look, my favorite, the shaved pubis. Pubic hair being so unruly and all. Very vain. This is a mockery, this is a sham, this is bullshit. Implants, collagen, plastics, capped teeth, the fat sucked out, the hair extended, the nose fixed, the bush shaved— these are not real women, all right? They're beauty freaks. And they make all us normal women with our wrinkles, our puckered boobs, our cellulite, seem somewhat inadequate. Well, I don't buy it, all right? What you fuckers, you think is that there's a chance in hell that you'll end up with one of these women, you don't give us real women anything approaching a commitment. It's pathetic. I don't know what you think you're going to do. You're going to end up eighty years old, drooling in some nursing home, and then you'll decide that it's time to settle down, get married, have kids? What are you going to do, find a cheerleader? . . . Look at Paul—with his models on the wall, his dog named Elle Macpherson. He's insane! He's obsessed. You're all obsessed. If you had an ounce of self-esteem, of self-worth, of self-confidence, you would realize that, as trite as it may sound, beauty is truly skin deep. And you know what? If you ever did hook one of those girls, I guarantee you'd be sick of her . . . No matter how perfect the nipple, how supple the thigh, unless there's some other shit going on in the relationship besides physical, it's going to get old, okay? And you guys, as a gender, have got to get a grip, otherwise the future of the human race is in jeopardy.

MAKING LOVE

Altered States, Paddy Chayefsky's final film, based on his novel, was directed by Ken Russell in a manner which way contributed to Chayefsky's heart attack—or so Paddy claimed. A brilliant screenplay remains. I won't take sides here, but experienced screenwriters will be familiar with the symptoms. Here is Chayefsky's last great take on life and love.

Emily: You make love with the fervor of a flagellant, Eddie, and while that has its satisfactions, sometimes I get the feeling it isn't me that's being made love to at all. I look up at you sometimes, and I get the feeling I'm being harpooned by some raging monk in the act of receiving God. So, you don't have to tell me how otherworldly you are. I know all about your need for an existential truth to replace the faith you abandoned at your father's deathbed. Well, human life doesn't have truth, Eddie. We're born screaming in doubt and we die suffocating in doubt, and human life consists of persuading ourselves we're actually alive. One of the ways we know we're alive is we love each other. Like I love you. I love you so much it hurts. I can't imagine living without you. So let's get married, and if it turns out to be a disaster, it'll be a disaster, and we'll shake hands and say goodbye.

INHIBITIONS

Now, Voyager's *Bette Davis has received a proposal of marriage. She'd like to be certain he's the right man.*

Charlotte: I'd like you to take me out to dinner some night this week, to some sort of bohemian place, and give me a very gay time—cocktails and champagne—and then make violent love to me. Then I'd know whether or not I could love you if I wasn't quite responsible. What I mean is, if I could only get rid of some of my inhibitions, just for once, I might be able to—to have more confidence. I don't know that I can tell you. But—well, I read about a woman, in a novel—a sort of repressed woman—who was in an automobile accident with a man. It was a very cold night, and they had to sit wrapped in a robe all night to keep warm. Just before they wrapped up, they both took a strong drink, and she fell in love with him because she lost her inhibitions. She was just—natural—you see. It sounds sort of depraved, I'm afraid.

Elliot: It certainly does! We're not that kind of people. Must we discuss such things, Charlotte?

Charlotte: No, Elliot. No. Not again.

Good news: she rejects his proposal.

INDECISION CENTRAL

In a film in which Sliding Doors *is a metaphor for fate (the train we just missed, or didn't), a woman waits for a man to make up his mind.*

Lydia: Don't you know, Jerry? Don't you know what I'm trying to do? I am trying to be your girlfriend, Jerry! I'm trying to win you back. It's fairly simple! I am standing on the platform at Limbo Central with my heart and soul packed in my suitcase, waiting for the Jerry-Freaking-Express to roll in and tell me that my ticket is still valid, that I may re-board the train. Only the station announcer keeps coming on and telling me that my train has been delayed, as the driver has suffered a major panic attack in Indecision City, we suggest you take the bus! That's what I'm trying to do, you cripple!

A COUPLE OF DOGS

Marty is the Chayefsky character who endeared himself to the world with this memorable exchange: "What do you want to do tonight?"—"I don't know, Angie, what do you want to do?" Marty breaks his solitude and our hearts, when he opens up to his girlfriend.

Marty: I think I'm a very nice guy. I also think I'm a pretty smart guy, in my own way. Now, I figure two people get married, and they gonna live together forty, fifty years. So it's just gotta be more than whether they're good-looking or not. You tell me you think you're not very good-looking. My father was a really ugly man, but my mother adored him. She told me that she used to get so miserable sometimes, like everybody, you know? And she says my father always tried to understand. I used to see them sometimes when I was a kid, sitting in the living room, talking and talking, and I used to adore my old man, because he was so kind. That's one of the most beautiful things I have in my life, the way my father and mother were. And my father was a real ugly man. So it doesn't matter if you look like a gorilla. So you see, dogs like us, we ain't such dogs as we think we are.

A SPURNED WIFE'S RESPONSE

Not one to allow the leads to have all the fun, Chayefsky gives a Network *news producer's wife the opportunity to respond to the news that her husband is having a midlife crisis, and has fallen for a young executive shark.*

Louise: . . . then get out, go to a hotel, go anywhere you want, go live with her, but don't come back! Because after twenty-five years of building a home and raising a family, and all the senseless pain we've inflicted on each other, I'll be damned if I'll just stand here and let you tell me you love somebody else! Because this isn't just some convention weekend with your secretary, is it? Or some broad you picked up after three belts of booze. This is your great winter romance, isn't it? Your last roar of passion before you sink into your emeritus years. Is that what's left for me? Is that my share? She gets the great winter passion and I get the dotage? Am I supposed to sit at home knitting and purling till you slink back like a penitent drunk? I'm your wife, damn it! If you can't work up a winter passion for me, then the least I require is respect and allegiance! I'm hurt! Don't you understand that? I'm hurt badly!

I'M ONE OF YOUR SCRIPTS

It doesn't work out so well for the producer and his girlfriend.

Max: It's the truth. After six months of living with you, I'm turning into one of your scripts. But this isn't a script, Diana. There's some real actual life going on here. I went to visit my wife today because she's in a state of depression, so depressed my daughter flew in from Seattle to be with her. And I feel lousy about that. I feel lousy about the pain I've caused my wife and kids. I feel guilty and conscience-stricken and all those things you think sentimental, but which my generation called simple human decency. And I miss my home because I'm beginning to get scared shitless. It's all suddenly closer to the end than to the beginning, and death is suddenly a perceptible thing to me, with definable features. You've got a man going through primal doubts, Diana, and you've got to cope with it. Because I'm not some guy discussing male menopause on the Barbara Walters show. I'm the man you presumably love. I live right here. I'm part of your life. I'm real. You can't switch to another channel.

TELEVISION INCARNATE

The generation gap between them is simply too great.

Max: It's too late, Diana! There's nothing left in you that I can live with! You're one of Howard's humanoids, and, if I stay with you, I'll be destroyed! Like Howard Beale was destroyed! Like Laureen Hobbs was destroyed! Like everything you and the institution of television touch is destroyed! You are television incarnate, Diana, indifferent to suffering, insensitive to joy. All of life is reduced to the common rubble of banality. War, murder, death, are all the same to you as bottles of beer. The daily business of life is a corrupt comedy. You even shatter the sensations of time and space into split-seconds and instant replays. You are madness, Diana, virulent madness, and everything you touch dies with you. Well, not me! Not while I can still feel pleasure and pain and love!

HAPPY ENDING

So Max decides to go back to his wife.

Max: It's a happy ending, Diana. Wayward husband comes to his senses, returns to his wife with whom he has built a long and sustaining love. Heartless young woman left alone in her arctic desolation. Music up with a swell. Final commercial. And here are a few scenes from next week's show.

THE NET CLOSES IN

This film has serious noir credits. Raymond Chandler wrote the screenplay from a novel by James Cain. Here Walter's boss, not knowing that he's talking to one of the murderers, describes what will give the killers away, killers who thought they had Double Indemnity.

Keyes: There it is, Walter. It's beginning to come apart at the seams already. A murder's never perfect. It always comes apart sooner or later. And when two people are involved it's usually sooner. We know the Dietrichson dame is in it, and somebody else. Pretty soon we're going to know who that somebody else is. He'll show. He's got to show. Sometime, somewhere, they've got to meet. Their emotions are all kicked up. Whether it's love or hate doesn't matter. They can't keep away from each other. They think it's twice as safe because there are two of them. But it's not twice as safe—it's ten times twice as dangerous. They've committed a murder, and that's not like taking a trolley ride together, where each one can get off at a different stop. They're stuck with each other. They've got to ride all the way to the end of the line. And it's a one-way trip, and the last stop is the cemetery.

I'M GAY

Think coming out of the closet is easy? Get Real.

Steven: I'm . . . I'm very proud, I'm very grateful to have won for the school. But I . . . I feel a bit of a fraud. You see, I wrote about growing up as how I imagined it must be for most of you but . . . there was another article which was to have been included in the school magazine. It was censored because it was about a young guy who just happened to be gay. I . . . I wrote that article. I wish you could have read it, so you could understand. Oh god, this is so hard. I'm sick of feeling totally alone, I want to have friends who like me for what I am, I want to be part of a family who loves me for who I am, not someone I pretend to be to keep their love. I'm sick of hiding, of being sad and scared. Have you got any idea? There must be more of you who feel like this, like I do. Why not just speak out? Thanks for proving my point. Well . . . I'm gay. Sorry Mum, Dad, but you can bet your life you're not the only parents out there with a gay son. It's only love, what's everyone so scared of? Thanks for listening.

WHAT IS LOVE?

Love can be Trouble Along the Way.

Steve Aloysius Williams: What do you know about love? Love is watching your child go off to school for the first time. Sitting beside a sick kid's bed, waiting for the doctor. Praying it isn't polio. Or that cold chill you get when you hear the screech of brakes, and you know your kid's outside on the street somewhere. And a lot of other things you can't get out of books, 'cause nobody knows how to write 'em down.

CHAPTER 12:

Other Passions

ON JOURNALISM

Another warm sentiment, this one from Meet Joe Black, *about the cowardly policies of the Rupert Murdochs of the world.*

Parrish: Umm—I did enjoy—or rather I was interested in, meeting John yesterday—Impressive . . . I suppose . . . But it did get me to thinking. I started in this business because this is what I wanted to do. I knew I wasn't going to write the Great American Novel, but I also knew there was more to life than buying something for a dollar and selling it for two. I wanted to give the news to the world, and I wanted to give it unvarnished. The more we all know about each other, the greater the chance we will survive. Sure, I want to make a profit, you can't exist without one, but John Bontecou is all profit. If we give him license to absorb Parrish Communications, and he has his eye on a few others after us, we'll be appointing him to the position he craves: Gatekeeper. In order to reach the world you will have to go through John Bontecou. And not only will you have to pay him to do this, far more expensive, you'll have to agree with him. Reporting the news is a privilege and a responsibility and it is not exploitable. Parrish Communications has earned this privilege, John Bontecou wants to buy it. As your chairman, I urge you to agree this company is not for sale.

ON FATHERHOOD

A Kramer vs. Kramer *is litigated across the country every day. Husbands might do more better in court if they were as eloquent as this one.*

Ted: When Joanna—my ex-wife—when she was talking before about how unhappy she was during our marriage . . . Well, I guess most of what she said was probably true. There were a lot of things I didn't understand—a lot of things I would do different if I could. Just like I guess there are a lot of things Joanna wishes she could change. But we can't. Some things, once they are done, can't be undone. Joanna says she loves Billy. I believe she does. So do I. But the way it was explained to me, that's not the issue. The only thing that's supposed to matter here is what's best for Billy . . .

When Joanna said, Why shouldn't a woman have the same ambitions as a man? I suppose she's right. But by the same token what law is it that says a woman is a better parent simply by virtue of sex? I guess I've had to think about whatever it is that makes somebody a good parent: constancy, patience, understanding . . . love. Where is it written that a man has any less of those qualities than a woman? Billy has a home with me, I've tried to make it the best I could. It's not perfect. I'm not a perfect parent. I don't have enough patience. Sometimes I forget he's just a little kid. But I love him. More than anything in this world I love him.

THE SON ALSO RISES

Now a son's point of view. This black man, about to marry a white girl against his father's advice, is going to live his own life, even if his father can Guess Who's Coming to Dinner?

John: You've said what you had to say—now you listen to me. You don't want to tell me how to live my life—so what do you think you're doing? You tell me what rights I've got or haven't got, and what I owe to you for what you did for me—and I will tell you now, I owe you nothing! If you carried that bag a million miles—you did what you were supposed to do! Because you brought me into this world, and from that day you owed me everything you could ever do for me, just as I will owe my kid—if I ever have any. But you don't own me. You can't tell me when or where I'm out of line, or try to make me live according to your rules—because you don't even know what I am. You don't know who I am—or what I believe or what I feel—and if I tried for the rest of my life, I couldn't explain it to you. You are thirty years older than I am, and your lousy generation believes that the way things were for you is the way they've got to be! And not until your whole generation has really lain down and died will the dead weight of you be off our backs! Don't you understand, you've got to be off my back! Dad, I haven't said this since I was a boy. But you're my father, and I'm your son, and I love you. I always have and I always will. But you, you think of yourself as a colored man. And I think of myself—as a man...

ON IMPOTENCE

Another great Paddy Chayefsky rant, this one by a middle-aged doctor who runs
The Hospital. He tells it like it is to a young, pretty hippie who's made a pass at
him, which he isn't sure he can reciprocate. (Unfortunately for the doc, the film
debuted before Viagra.)

Bock: What the hell's wrong with being impotent? My God, you kids are
more hung up on sex than the Victorians! I have a son, twenty-three. I
threw him out of the house last year. Pietistic little humbug. He preached
universal love and despised everyone. He had a blanket contempt for
the middle class, even its decencies. He detested my mother because
she took such *petit bourgeois* pride in her son, the doctor. I cannot tell you
how brutishly he ignored that rather good old lady. When she died, he
refused to go to the funeral. He thought the chapel service a hypocrisy.
His generation didn't live with lies, he told me. Everybody lives with lies,
I said. I grabbed him by his poncho, dragged him the full length of our
seven-room, despicably affluent middle-class apartment and flung him
out. I haven't seen him since. But do you know what he said to me as he
stood there on that landing, on the verge of tears? He shrieked at me, "You
old fink! You can't even get it up anymore!" That was it, you see. That was
his real revolution. It wasn't racism and the oppressed poor and the war
in Vietnam. The ultimate American societal sickness was a limp dingus.
Hah! By God, if there is a despised and misunderstood minority in this
country, it's us poor impotent bastards. Well, I'm impotent and proud of it!
Impotence is beautiful, baby! Power to the impotent! Right on, baby! . . .
when I say impotent, I don't mean merely limp. Disagreeable as it may be
for a woman, a man may sometimes lust for other things, something less
transient than an erection, some sense of permanent worth. That's what
medicine is for me, a *raison d'etre*. When I was thirty-four, Miss Drummond,
I presented a paper before the annual convention of the Society of Clinical
Investigation that pioneered the whole goddamn field of immunology. A
breakthrough! I'm in all the textbooks. I happen to be an eminent man,
Miss Drummond. And you want to know something, Miss Drummond?
I don't give a damn. When I say I'm impotent, I mean I've lost even my
desire for work, which is a hell of a lot more primal a passion than sex.

I've lost my *raison d'etre*, my purpose, the only thing I ever truly loved. It's all rubbish, anyway. Transplants, anti-bodies, we manufacture genes, we can produce birth ectogenetically, we can practically clone people like carrots, and half the kids in this ghetto haven't even been inoculated for polio! We have assembled the most enormous medical establishment ever conceived, and people are sicker than ever! We cure nothing! We heal nothing! The whole goddamn wretched world is strangulating in front of our eyes! That's what I mean when I say "impotence!" You don't know what the hell I'm talking about, do you?

ON MUSIC

Fans of music will sympathize with the strong feelings of an old-time jazz man.

Elwood Blues: You may go if you wish, but remember this: walk away now, and you walk away from your crafts, your skills, your vocations, leaving the next generation with nothing but recycled, digitally sampled techno-grooves, quasi-synth rhythms, pseudo songs of violence-laden gangsta rap, acid pop, and simpering, ciphering, soulless slush. Depart now, and you forever separate yourselves from the vital American legacies of Robert Johnson, Muddy Waters, Willie Dickson, Jimmy Reed, Memphis Slim, Blind Boy Fuller, Louie Jordan, Little Walter, Big Walter, Sonny Boy Williamson I and II, Otis Redding, Jackie Wilson, Elvis Presley, Lieber and Stoller, and Robert K. Weiss. Turn your backs now and you snuff out the fragile candles of blues, R&B and soul. And when those flames flicker and expire, the light of the world is extinguished, because the music which has moved mankind for seven decades leading to the millennium will wither and die on the vine of abandonment and neglect.

ON HATRED

Bigotry, as described in Mississippi Burning *by a son and then a wife, has its causes. Here are two.*

Rupert: You know, when I was a little boy, there was an old negro farmer that lived down the road from us, name of Monroe. And he was, I guess he was just a little luckier than my daddy was. He bought himself a mule. That was a big deal around that town. Now, my daddy hated that mule because his friends were always kidding him about how they saw Monroe out plowing with his new mule, and Monroe was going to rent another field now that he had a mule. One morning that mule just showed up dead. They poisoned the water. And after that there was never any mention about that mule around my daddy. Just never came up. 'Til one time we were driving down the road, and we passed Monroe's place and we saw it was empty. He just packed up and left, I guess. Gone up north or something. I looked over at my daddy's face and I knew he'd done it, and he saw that I knew. He was ashamed. I guess he was ashamed. And he looked at me and he said, "If you ain't better than a nigger, son, then who are you better than?" . . . An old man who was just so full of hate that he didn't know that being poor was what was killing him.

And . . .

Mrs. Pell: It's not good for you to be here. It's ugly. This whole thing is so ugly. Have you any idea what it's like to live with this? People look at us and all they see is bigots and racists. Hatred isn't something you're born with—It gets taught. At school they said segregation is what's said in the Bible. Genesis nine, verse twenty-seven. At seven years of age you get told it enough times, you believe it. You believe the hatred. You live it. You breathe it. You marry it . . . My husband drove one of the cars that night. That's what you want to hear, isn't it? The bodies are buried on the Roberts farm in an earthen dam.

CHAPTER 13:

Back to the Future

WHY WE'RE HERE

In the future (known throughout the twentieth century as 2001), a HAL-9000 computer takes over the spaceship S.S. Discovery, killing all but one of the crew. While trying to determine what went wrong, surviving astronaut Dave Bowman tracks down this message from the original project commander and hears the history of eternity.

Voice: Thirteen months before the launch date of your Saturn mission, on April 12th, 2001, the first evidence for intelligent life outside the Earth was discovered. It was found buried at a depth of fifteen meters in the crater Tycho. No news of this was ever announced, and the event had been kept secret since then, for reasons which I will later explain. Soon after it was uncovered, it emitted a powerful blast of radiation in the radio spectrum, which seems to have been triggered by the Lunar sunrise. Luckily for those at the site, it proved harmless. Perhaps you can imagine our astonishment when we later found it was aimed precisely at Saturn. A lot of thought went into the question of whether or not it was sun-triggered, as it seemed illogical to deliberately bury a sun-powered device. Burying it could only shield it from the sun, since its intense magnetic field made it otherwise easily detectable. We finally concluded that the only reason you might bury a sun-powered device would be to keep it inactive until it would be uncovered, at which time it would absorb sunlight and trigger itself. What is its purpose? I wish we knew. The object was buried on the moon about four million years ago, when our ancestors were primitive man-apes. We've examined dozens of theories, but the one that has the most currency at the moment is that the object serves as an alarm. What the purpose of the alarm is, why they wish to have the alarm, whether the alarm represents any danger to us—these are questions no one can answer. The intentions of an alien world at least four million years older than we are cannot be reliably predicted. In view of this, the intelligence and scientific communities felt that any public announcement might lead to significant cultural shock and disorientation. Discussion took place at the highest levels between governments, and it was decided that the only wise and precautionary course to follow was to assume that the intentions of this alien world are potentially dangerous to us, until we have evidence to the contrary. This is, of course, why security has been maintained and why this information has been kept on a need-to-know basis. And now I should like to show you a TV monitor tape of the actual signaling event. For two million years it had circled Saturn, awaiting a moment of destiny that might never come. In its making, the moon had been shattered and, around the central world, the debris of its creation orbited yet—the glory and the enigma of the solar system. Now the long wait was ending. On yet another world, intelligence had been born and was escaping from its planetary cradle. An ancient experiment was about to reach its climax. Those who had begun the experiment so long ago had not been men. But when they looked out across the depths of space, they felt awe and wonder— and loneliness. In their explorations, they encountered life in many forms, and watched on a thousand worlds the workings of evolution. They saw how often the first faint sparks of intelligence flickered and died in the cosmic night. And because, in all the galaxy, they had found nothing more precious than Mind, they encouraged its dawning everywhere. The great dinosaurs had long since perished when their ships entered the solar system, after a voyage that had already lasted thousands of years. They swept past the frozen outer planets, paused briefly above the deserts of dying Mars and presently looked down on Earth. For years they studied, collected and catalogued. When they had learned all they could, they began to modify. They tinkered with the destiny of many species on land and in the ocean, but which of their experiments would succeed they could not know for at least a million years. They were patient but they were not yet immortal. There was much to do in this universe of a hundred billion stars. So they set forth once more across the abyss, knowing that they would never come this way again. Nor was there any need. Their wonderful machines could be trusted to do the rest. On Earth, the glaciers came and went while, above them, the changeless Moon still carried its secret. With a yet slower rhythm than the polar ice, the tide of civilization ebbed and flowed across the galaxy. Strange and beautiful and terrible empires rose and fell, and passed on their knowledge to their successors. Earth was not forgotten, but it was one of a million silent worlds, few of which would ever speak. Then the first explorers of Earth, recognizing the limitations of their minds and bodies, passed on their knowledge to the great machines they had created, and who now transcended them in every way. For a few thousand years, they shared their universe with their machine children. Then, realizing that it was folly to linger when their task was done, they passed into history without regret. Not one of them ever looked through his own eyes upon the planet Earth again. But even the age of the Machine Entities passed swiftly. In their ceaseless experimenting, they had learned to store knowledge in the structure of space itself, and to preserve their thoughts for eternity in frozen lattices of light. They could become creatures of radiation, free at last from the tyranny of matter. Now they were lords of the galaxy, and beyond the reach of time. They could rove at will among the stars and sink like a subtle mist through the very interstices of space. But despite their god-like powers, they still watched over the experiments their ancestors had started so many generations ago. The companion of Saturn knew nothing of this, as it orbited in its no man's land between Mimas and the outer edge of rings. It had only to remember and wait, and to look forever sunward with its strange senses. For many weeks it had watched the approaching ship. Its long-dead makers had prepared it for many things, and this was one of them. And it recognized what was climbing starward from the Sun. If it had been alive, it would have felt excitement, but such an emotion was irrelevant to its great powers. Even if the ship had passed it by, it would not have known the slightest trace of disappointment. It had waited four million years; it was prepared to wait for eternity. Presently, it felt the gentle touch of radiations trying to probe its secrets. Now the ship was in orbit, and it began to speak with prime numbers from one to eleven, over and over again. Soon these gave way to more complex signals at many frequencies, ultra-violet, infra-red, X-rays. The machine made no reply. It had nothing to say. Then it saw the first robot probe, which descended and hovered above the chasm. Then it dropped into darkness. The great machine knew that this tiny scout was reporting back to its parent, but it was too simple, too primitive a device to detect the forces that were gathering 'round it now. Then the pod came, carrying life. The great machine searched its memories. The logic circuits made their decision when the pod had fallen beyond the last faint glow of the reflected Saturnian light. In a moment of time, too short to be measured, space turned and twisted upon itself.

VIRTUAL LIFE

Here's a less benign vision of the future: machines instead of humans, all living in The Matrix.

Morpheus: Do you want to know what it is, Neo? It's that feeling you have had all your life. That feeling that something was wrong with the world. You don't know what it is but it's there, like a splinter in your mind, driving you mad, driving you to me. But what is it? The Matrix is everywhere, it's all around us, here even in this room. You can see it out your window, or on your television. You feel it when you go to work, or go to church or pay your taxes. It is the world that has been pulled over your eyes to blind you from the truth. That you are a slave, Neo. That you, like everyone else, were born into bondage . . . kept inside a prison that you cannot smell, taste, or touch. A prison for your mind. Unfortunately, no one can be told what the Matrix is. You have to see it for yourself.

Epilogue

LIFE FLASHES BY

This hero, dying, leaves us with an impression of American Beauty.

Lester: I had always heard your entire life flashes in front of your eyes the second before you die. First of all, that one second isn't a second at all, it stretches forever, like an ocean of time. For me, it was lying on my back at Boy Scout camp, watching falling stars . . . and yellow leaves from the maple trees that lined my street . . . Or my grandmother's hands, and the way her skin seemed like paper . . . and the first time I saw my cousin Tony's brand new Firebird. And Janie . . . and Janie. And . . . Carolyn. I guess I could be really pissed off about what happened to me, but it's hard to stay mad when there's so much beauty in the world. Sometimes I feel like I'm seeing it all at once, and it's too much, my heart fills up like a balloon that's about to burst, and then I remember to relax and stop trying to hold on to it, and then it flows through me like rain. And I can't feel anything but gratitude for every single moment of my stupid little life. You have no idea what I'm talking about, I'm sure. But don't worry. You will someday.

THE BIG SLEEP

The father of pulp fiction and noir language, Raymond Chandler, here adapted by William Faulkner and others, discusses The Big Sleep.

Phillip Marlowe: What did it matter where you lay once you were dead? In a dirty sump, or in a marble tower on the top of a high hill? You were dead, you were sleeping the big sleep, you were not bothered by things like that. Oil and water were the same as wind and air to you. You just slept the big sleep, not caring about the nastiness of how you died or where you fell. Me, I was part of the nastiness now. Far more a part of it than Rusty Regan was. But the old man didn't have to be. He could lie quiet in his canopied bed, with his bloodless hands folded on the sheet, waiting. His heart was a brief, uncertain murmur. His thoughts were as gray as ashes. And in a little while he, too, like Rusty Regan, would be sleeping the big sleep.

THERE'S NOTHING TO KNOW

And finally, from Get Shorty . . .

Chili: You know how to write one of these?

Bo Catlett: There's nothin' to know. You have an idea, you write down what you wanna say. Then you get somebody to add in the commas and shit where they belong, if you aren't positive yourself. Maybe fix up the spelling where you have some tricky words, although I've seen scripts where I know words weren't spelled right, and there was hardly any commas in it at all. So I don't think it's too important. Anyway, you come to the last page you write in "Fade out" and that's the end, you're done.

Chili: That's all there is to it, huh?

Bo Catlett: That's all.

Chili: Then what do I need you for?

CREDITS

FILM	SCREENPLAY BY
2001: A Space Odyssey	Stanley Kubrick & Arthur C. Clarke
42nd Street	Rian James & James Seymour, based on the novel by Bradford Ropes
The Alamo	James Edward Grant
All Quiet on the Western Front	George Abbott, Maxwell Anderson, and Dell Andrews, based on the novel by Erich Maria Remarque
All the President's Men	William Goldman, based on the book by Carl Bernstein and Bob Woodward
All That Jazz	Robert Aurthur & Bob Fosse
Altered States	Paddy Chayefsky (under the pseudonym Sidney Aaron)
American Beauty	Alan Ball
The Americanization of Emily	Paddy Chayefsky, based on the novel by William Bradford Huie
An American in Paris	Alan Jay Lerner
...And Justice for All	Valerie Curtin & Barry Levinson
Andy Hardy's Blonde Trouble	Aurania Rouverol (characters), Harry Ruskin (screenplay) & William Ludwig (screenplay) and Agnes Christine Johnston (screenplay)

Animal Crackers	Morrie Ryskind, based on the play by Bert Kalmar, George S. Kaufman, Harry Ruby & Morrie Ryskind
Annie Hall	Woody Allen & Marshall Brickman
Any Given Sunday	John Logan and Oliver Stone, story by Daniel Pyne and John Logan
Apocalypse Now	Francis Ford Coppola and John Milus, based on the novel *Heart of Darkness* by Joseph Conrad, narration by Michael Herr
As Good As It Gets	Mark Andrus and James Brooks, story by Mark Andrus
The Asphalt Jungle	Ben Maddow and John Huston, based on the novel by W. R. Burnett
Austin Powers: International Man of Mystery	Mike Myers. "Austin Powers: International Man of Mystery" © MCMXCVII New Line Productions, Inc. All rights reserved. Dialogue appears courtesy of New Line Productions, Inc.
The Bad and the Beautiful	Charles Schnee, based on the story "Tribute to a Badman" by George Bradshaw
Battleground	Robert Pirosh
Beautiful Girls	Scott Michael Rosenberg

The Big Chill	Barbara Benedek & Lawrence Kasdan
The Big Sleep	William Faulkner, Leigh Brackett, and Jules Furthman, based on the novel by Raymond Chandler
Blues Brothers 2000	Dan Aykroyd & John Landis
The Boiler Room	Ben Younger. "Boiler Room" © MM New Line Productions, Inc. All rights reserved. Dialogue appears courtesy of New Line Productions, Inc.
Bonnie and Clyde	David Newman & Robert Benton
Bram Stoker's Dracula	James V. Hart, based on the novel by Bram Stoker
Bringing Up Baby	Dudley Nichols & Hagar Wilde, story by Hagar Wilde
Bull Durham	Ron Shelton
Carefree	Allan Scott and Ernest Pagano, based on the story by Marian Ainslee, Guy Endore, and Dudley Nichols
Citizen Kane	Herman J. Mankiewicz and Orson Welles
Coming Home	Nancy Dowd, Robert C. Jones, Waldo Salt
Curse of the Cat People	DeWitt Bodeen
Dead Poets Society	Tom Schulman

The Devil and Daniel Webster	Dan Totheroh and Stephen Vincent Benet, based on "The Devil and Daniel Webster" by Stephen Vincent Benet
Devil's Advocate	Jonathan Lemkin and Tony Gilroy, based on the novel by Andrew Neiderman
Double Indemnity	Billy Wilder and Raymond Chandler, based on the story *Double Indemnity* by James M. Cain
Dr. Strangelove, or: How I Learned to Stop Worrying and Love the Bomb	Stanley Kubrick and Terry Southern & Peter George, based on the novel *Red Alert* by Peter George
Dracula	Baltazar Fernández Cué, based on the play by Hamilton Deane and Garret Fort, and the novel by Bram Stoker
The Elephant Man	Eric Bergren, Christopher De Vore, David Lynch, based on the books *The Elephant Man and Other Reminisces* by Frederick Treves and *The Elephant Man: A Study in Human Dignity* by Ashley Montagu
A Few Good Men	Aaron Sorkin, based on his play
Field of Dreams	Phil Alden Robinson, based on the novel by W.P Kinsella
The Fifth Element	Luc Besson & Robert Mark Kamen, based on the story by Luc Besson

The Fight for Life	Pare Lorentz, adapted from the "Maternal Welfare" chapters of *The Fight for Life* by Paul de Kruif
The Fisher King	Richard LaGravenese
Get Real	Patrick Wilde
Get Shorty	Scott Frank, based on the novel by Elmore Leonard
Gilda	Marion Parsonnet and Ben Hecht (uncredited), adaptation by Jo Eisinger, story by E.A. Ellington
Gladiator	David Franzoni and John Logan and William Nicholson, based on a story by David Franzoni
Glen or Glenda?	Edward D. Wood, Jr.
The Goddess	Paddy Chayefsky
Good Will Hunting	Matt Damon & Ben Affleck
The Great Dictator	Charles Chaplin
Guess Who's Coming to Dinner	William Rose
Guys and Dolls	Joseph L. Mankiewicz, based on the play by Abe Burrows and Jo Swerling, based on the story "The Idyll of Miss Sarah Brown" by Damon Runyon
Harold and Maude	Colin Higgins

High Noon	Carl Foreman, story "The Tin Star" by John W. Cunningham
The Hospital	Paddy Chayefsky
It's a Wonderful Life	Frances Goodrich & Albert Hackett and Frank Capra, additional scenes by Jo Swerling, based on the short story "The Greatest Gift" by Philip Van Doren Stern
Judgment at Nuremberg	Abby Mann, based on the story by Abby Mann
Kids	Harmony Korine and Jim Lewis, story by Larry Clark and Leo Fitzpatrick
Kramer vs. Kramer	Robert Benton, based on the novel by Avery Corman
The Lady Eve	Preston Sturges, story by Monckton Hoffe
The Life of Emile Zola	Heinz Herald, Geza Herczeg, Norman Reilly Raine, based on *Zola and His Time* by Matthew Josephson
Lilith	Robert Rossen, based on the novel by J.R. Salamanca
Little Big Man	Calder Willingham, based on the novel by Thomas Berger
Lost Horizon	Robert Riskin, based on the novel by James Hilton

The Lost Weekend	Charles Bracket and Billy Wilder, based on the novel by Charles R. Jackson
M	Thea von Harbou and Fritz Lang, based on an article by Egon Jacobson
The Magnificent Seven	William Roberts & Walter Bernstein, based on the film "The Seven Samurai" by Akira Kurosawa
Malice	Aaron Sorkin and Scott Frank, story by Aaron Sorkin & Jonas McCord
The Maltese Falcon	John Huston, based on the novel by Dashiell Hammet
Marty	Paddy Chayefsky, based on his teleplay
The Matrix	Andy Wachowski, Larry Wachowski
Meet Joe Black	Ron Osborn & Jeff Reno and Kevin Wade and Bo Goldman, based on the play *Death Takes a Holiday* by Alberto Casella, adaptation by Walter Ferris, from the 1934 screenplay by Maxwell Anderson and Gladys Lehman
Meet John Doe	Robert Riskin, based on a story by Richard Connell and Robert Presnell, Sr.
The Miracle of Morgan's Creek	Preston Sturges
Mississippi Burning	Chris Gerolmo, based on the book *Three Lives for Mississippi* by William Bradford Huie

Mr. Smith Goes to Washington	Sidney Buchman & Lewis R. Foster
The Naked City	Albert Maltz and Malvin Wald, based on a story by Malvin Wald
Network	Paddy Chayefsky
Ninotchka	Charles Brakett, Billy Wilder, and Walter Reisch, story by Melchior Lengyel
Notting Hill	Richard Curtis
Now, Voyager	Casey Robinson, based on the novel by Olive Higgins Prouty
Out of Africa	Kurt Luedtke, based on the books *Out of Africa, Shadows on the Grass*, and *Letters from Africa* by Isak Dinesen, the book *Isak Dinesen: The Life of a Storyteller* by Judith Thurman, and the book *Silence Will Speak* by Errol Trzebinski
The Palm Beach Story	Preston Sturges
The Pawnbroker	Morton S. Fine, David Friedkin, based on the novel by Edward Lewis Wallant
Philadelphia	Ron Nyswaner
Platoon	Oliver Stone
The Player	Michael Tolkin, based on his novel
Psycho	Joseph Stefano, based on the novel by Robert Bloch
San Francisco	Anita Loos, story by Robert E. Hopkins

Scarface	Oliver Stone (with an uncredited nod to the 1932 screenplay by Howard Hawks and the novel by Armitage Trail, a.k.a. Maurice Coons)
Sea of Love	Richard Price
Shakespeare in Love	Marc Norman and Tom Stoppard
Sliding Doors	Peter Howitt
Stagecoach	Dudley Nichols, Ben Hecht (uncredited), based on the short story "Stage to Lordsburg" by Ernest Haycox
Star Trek IV: The Voyage Home	Steve Meerson & Peter Krikes and Harve Bennett & Nicholas Meyer, story by Leonard Nimoy & Harve Bennett
The Story of Louis Pasteur	Sheridan Gibney and Pierre Collings, based on a story by Pierre Collings and Sheridan Gibney
Sullivan's Travels	Preston Sturges
Sunset Boulevard	Charles Brackett, Billy Wilder, and D.M. Marshman, Jr.
Swimming with Sharks	George Huang
Talk Radio	Oliver Stone and Eric Bogosian, based on the play by Eric Bogosian & Ted Savinar, and the book *Talked to Death: The Life and Murder of Alan Berg* by Stephen Singular
This Land Is Mine	Dudley Nichols

Tin Men	Barry Levinson
Treasure of the Sierra Madre	John Huston, based on the novel by B. Traven
Trouble Along the Way	Jack Rose, Melville Shavelson, based on the story by Robert Hardy Andrews and Douglas Morrow
Tucker: The Man and His Dream	Arnold Schulman, David Seidler
Twelve Monkeys	David Webb Peoples & Janet Peoples, based on the film *La Jetée* by Chris Marker
Up the Down Staircase	Tad Mosel, based on the novel by Bel Kaufman
Watch on the Rhine	Dashiell Hammet, based on the play by Lillian Hellman, with additional scenes and dialogue by Lillian Hellman
What Price Hollywood?	Gene Fowler, Rowland Brown, based on a story by Adela Rogers St. Johns, and a screenplay by Jane Murtin, Ben Markson, and Alan Rivkin, with an adaptation by Robert Presnell, Sr.
When Harry Met Sally	Nora Ephron
The Witches of Eastwick	Michael Cristofer, based on the novel by John Updike
Without Reservations	Andrew Solt, based on the novel *Thanks, God! I'll Take It from Here* by Jane Allen & Mae Livingston

Yankee Doodle Dandy   Robert Buckner and Edmund Joseph,
                                additional material by Julius and
                                Philip Epstein, original story by
                                Robert Buckner

TEXT AND PHOTOGRAPH PERMISSIONS

The speeches included in this book appear courtesy of the following:

Disney: *Dead Poets Society*; *Tin Men*.

DreamWorks: *American Beauty*. The Shooting Script ® screenplay and Afterword by Alan Ball, Introduction by Sam Mendes, design copyright © 1999 by Newmarket Press. Trademark and © 1999 DreamWorks. All rights reserved. Reprinted by permission of Newmarket Press, 18 East 48th Street, New York, NY 10017. *Gladiator*.

Lucasfilm: *Tucker: The Man and His Dream*.

MGM: *2001: A Space Odyssey*; *The Alamo*; *An American in Paris*; *The Americanization of Emily*; *Andy Hardy's Blonde Trouble*; *Annie Hall*; *Apocalypse Now*; *The Asphalt Jungle*; *The Bad and the Beautiful*; *Battleground*; *Bull Durham*; *Coming Home*; *Get Shorty*; *The Great Dictator*; *Guys and Dolls*; *High Noon*; *The Hospital*; *Judgment at Nuremberg*; *The Magnificent Seven*; *Marty*; *Mississippi Burning*; *Network*; *Ninotchka*; *The Pawnbroker*; *San Francisco*; *Stagecoach*.

Miramax Films: *Beautiful Girls*. Courtesy of Miramax Film Corp. All rights reserved. *Good Will Hunting*. Courtesy of Miramax Film Corp. All rights reserved. *Shakespeare in Love*. Courtesy of Miramax Film Corp. All rights reserved.

New Line Productions: *Austin Powers: International Man of Mystery*. Copyright © MCMXCVII New Line Productions, Inc. All rights reserved. Dialogue appears courtesy of New Line Productions, Inc. *The Boiler Room*. Copyright © MM New Line Productions, Inc. All rights reserved. Dialogue appears courtesy of New Line Productions, Inc.

Paramount Pictures: *Harold and Maude*; *It's a Wonderful Life*; *The Miracle of Morgan's Creek*; *Star Trek IV: The Voyage Home*; *Sunset Boulevard*.

Sony Pictures: *A Few Good Men*; *All That Jazz*; *As Good As It Gets*; *The Big Chill*; *Bram Stoker's Dracula*; *Dr. Strangelove, or: How I Learned to Stop Worrying and Love the Bomb*; *The Fisher King*; *Gilda*; *The Goddess*; *Guess Who's Coming to Dinner*; *Kramer vs. Kramer*; *Lilith*; *Lost Horizon*; *Malice*; *Mr. Smith Goes to Washington*; *Philadelphia*.

Universal Pictures: *All Quiet on the Western Front*; *Animal Crackers*; *Blues Brothers 2000*; *Curse of the Cat People*; *The Devil and Daniel Webster*; *Double Indemnity*; *Dracula*; *The Elephant Man*; *Field of Dreams*; *The Fifth Element*; *The Lady Eve*; *The Lost Weekend*; *Meet Joe Black*; *The Naked City*; *Out of Africa*; *The Palm Beach Story*; *Psycho*; *Scarface*; *Sea of Love*; *Sullivan's Travels*; *Talk Radio*; *Twelve Monkeys*.

Warner Brothers: *42nd Street*; *All the President's Men*; *Any Given Sunday*; *The Big Sleep*; *Bonnie and Clyde*; *Bringing Up Baby*; *Carefree*; *Citizen Kane*; *Devil's Advocate*; *The Life of Emile Zola*; *The Maltese Falcon*; *The Matrix*; *Meet John Doe*; *Now, Voyager*; *The Story of Louis Pasteur*; *This Land Is Mine*; *Treasure of the Sierra Madre*; *Trouble Along the Way Up the Down Staircase*; *Watch on the Rhine*; *What Price Hollywood?*; *When Harry Met Sally*; *Yankee Doodle Dandy*.

The photographs reproduced in this book are from the following sources:

Photofest: Russell Crowe in *Gladiator*, cover; Gloria Swanson in *Sunset Boulevard*, pg. vii and cover; Tim Robbins and Susan Sarandon in *Bull Durham*, pg. 3; Chief Dan George and Dustin Hoffman in *Little Big Man*, pg. 20; John Wayne in *Stagecoach*, pg. 28; Orson Welles in *Citizen Kane*, pg. 39; Greta Garbo in *Ninotchka*, pg. 44 and cover; Bella Lugosi in *Dracula*, pg. 47 and cover; Ray Milland in *The Lost Weekend*, pg. 49; Michael Myers in *Austin Powers: International Man of Mystery*, pg. 51; "Mother" in *Psycho*, pg. 55; Gene Kelly in *An American in Paris*, pg. 60; Peter Sellers and Sterling Hayden in *Dr. Strangelove, or: How I Learned to Stop Worrying and Love the Bomb*, pg. 86 and cover; Paul Muni in *The Life of Emile Zola*, pg. 111; John Wayne in *The Alamo*, pg. 119 and cover; Groucho Marx in *Animal Crackers*, pg. 123; Tim Robbins in *The Player*, pg. 133; Jack Nicholson in *The Witches of Eastwick*, pg. 149 and cover; Dan Aykroyd and Jim Belushi in *The Blues Brothers 2000*, pg. 165.

Author's collection: Sam Jaffe in *Lost Horizon*, pg. 13; Al Puccino in *...And Justice for All*, pg. 17; Robin Williams in *Good Will Hunting*, pg. 19; Fred Astaire in *Carefree*, pg. 22; Humphrey Bogart in *The Maltese Falcon*, pg. 24; Rod Steiger in *The Pawnbroker*, pg. 43; Alec Baldwin in *Malice*, pg. 45; Peter Lorre in *M*, pg. 56; Spencer Tracy in *Judgment at Nuremberg*, pg. 81, Charlie Chaplin in *The Great Dictator*, pg. 83; Jack Nicholson in *A Few Good Men*, pg. 85; Peter Finch in *Network*, pg. 102; James Stewart in *Mr. Smith Goes to Washington*, pg. 113; Jeff Bridges in *Tucker: The Man and His Dream*, pg. 117; Joseph Fiennes in *Shakespeare in Love*, pg. 139; John Hurt and Anne Bancroft in *The Elephant Man*, pg. 140; Robin Williams in *The Fisher King*, pg. 145.